The Religious Revolution

in the Ivory Coast

The University of North Carolina Press   Chapel Hill

Sheila S. Walker

THE RELIGIOUS REVOLUTION IN THE IVORY COAST

The Prophet Harris and
the Harrist Church

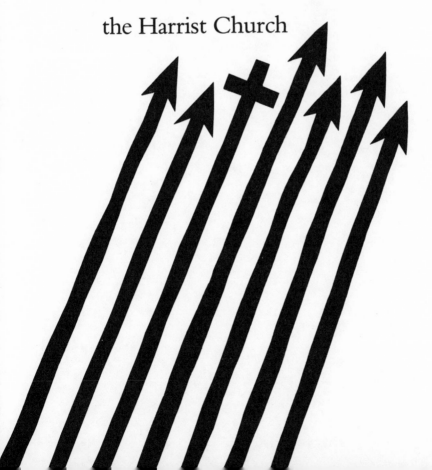

© 1983 The University of North Carolina Press
Manufactured in the United States of America

Library of Congress Cataloging in Publication Data

Walker, Sheila S.
    The religious revolution in the Ivory Coast.

    (Studies in religion)
    Bibliography: p.
    Includes index.
    1. Harris, William Wade.   2. Ivory Coast—Church
history.   I. Title.   II. Series: Studies in religion
(Chapel Hill, N.C.)
BV3785.H348W34   289'.9   81-13010
ISBN 0-8078-1503-9   AACR2

To my father, James Walker,
my mother, Susan Snell, and
my husband, Terry Brown, and
to the proud members of the Harrist
Church of the Ivory Coast

Contents

vii

Contents | ix

Preface

I did the field research for this study of the origins, development, and present status of the Harrist Church of the Ivory Coast during an eighteen-month stay in the country in 1971–72, making follow-up visits in 1974 and 1979. The field research was focused on the lagoons villages around Abidjan, capital of the Ivory Coast, where the religion was created and remains most concentrated and influential. Information on the church was gathered from personal observation and participation in church and village activities, and from discussions with old and young Harrists and with other Ivorians who are not members of the church. These data were supplemented by information from historical documents found in the National Archives of the Ivory Coast and from the writings mainly of missionaries and colonial administrators concerning the beginnings of the movement, and of scholars and journalists who have shown an interest in this religious phenomenon over the years. Throughout the book, statements concerning the Harrist church that are not referenced to written sources are part of Harrist oral tradition, gathered from many Harrists in interviews and discussions during the field work. Statements and descriptions are not usually attributed to specific individuals, both to protect their anonymity and because many people corroborated the information.

The many Harrists who were very kind and helpful to me I cannot, unfortunately, cite by name to thank, but I am very grateful to them all, and hope that my work may be somehow useful to them in the further evolution of their church. I would like to extend special and individual thanks to the founder and patriarch of the Harrist Church, John Ahui, and to his son and supporter, Paul Ahui; and also to Ernest Amos-Djoro, who made available to me valuable unpublished material on the Harrist church; to Abraham Nandjui, President of the Methodist Church of the Ivory Coast, who indicated that all Ivorian Christians owed a debt to the Prophet

Harris; to Bruno Claver, dedicated Harrist leader; to Daniel Boadi and his family, great friends who spent a great deal of time explaining their religion to me; to Minister Bruno Abéto and the young men in the choir of the Harrist Church in Abobo-Doumé, who treated me like an honorary Harrist; and to Claude Pairrault and René Bureau, then of the Faculté d'Ethnosociologie at the University of Abidjan, who facilitated my research efforts. On this side of the ocean I am grateful for their support at different phases in the development of this book to Charles Long, William Shack, Elliot Skinner, and Preston Williams.

My greatest gratitude is to my husband, Terry Brown, who tolerated me through the entire process of making this book a reality; and to my good friend Jeanne Bunderson Ewing, who began just typing the manuscript, but then got involved in the content and gave me valuable feedback that helped me develop the guiding ideas of the book.

Introduction

The story of the Christianization of the Ivory Coast began in 1913 with the arrival in the colony of the native Liberian prophet William Wade Harris. Harris traveled to the Ivory Coast to pursue the mission with which he believed God had charged him— that of converting the African populations to Christianity. His efforts inspired a multiethnic mass movement that swept the southern region of the country. The Prophet Harris influenced more people in the Ivory Coast than any other historical figure until Félix Houphouet-Boigny, who later became the independent nation's first president, came to power in the nationalist period of the 1940s.

At the time of the 1921 census, the Ivory Coast colony had a population of 1,544,845 (Bianquis 1924: 1086). Within a few months, Harris increased the number of Christians from the few hundred converted by Catholic missionaries to more than 100,000, or almost one-tenth of the entire population of the country. Harris's extraordinary movement, which revolutionized the religious life of most of the southern portion of the country, has been described by missionaries as "a tidal wave of Christianity rolling across the country." A French colonial administrator characterized the movement as "an almost unbelievable religious event that upset all of the ideas that we had about the primitive, rustic black societies of the coast, which will be, with our occupation, the most important political and social event of ten centuries of past, present, or future history of the maritime Ivory Coast" (Marty 1922: 13).

Indeed, "Harrism," as the same official characterized the movement, did represent the "takeoff" of Christianity in the country (Marty 1922: 13). Whereas the missionaries summoned by the colonial administration had been singularly unsuccessful in their efforts to replace the indigenous religions with Christianity, Harris accomplished the task in a matter of months. Of the people he converted, one group joined the Catholic church, a second group became Protestant, and a third group founded the Harrist Church of the Ivory Coast, one of the largest African Christian churches on the continent, and the most original in its beginnings and development.

The approximately 5 million members of the Ivorian population are currently divided into an estimated 100,000 Harrists, 200,000 Protestants, 500,000 Catholics, and 1 million Muslims, with the majority of the population maintaining their indigenous religions. A small minority belongs to other new religious institutions that grew out of the Harrist movement.[1] As a result, one-seventh of the Christians in the Ivory Coast are Harrists, and the Prophet Harris was influential in determining the current religious orientation of more than 16 percent of the entire population of the country.

The Harrist church is one of the African Christian churches that John Mbiti characterized as "the most serious religious phenomenon in modern Africa." He estimated that at least one-fifth of all African Christians are members of such churches (Mbiti 1970: 303–4). David Barrett has indicated that as of 1967 there were 5,000 distinct and separately evolved independent religious bodies in thirty-four African nations, with a total membership of over 7 million people.[2] Since 1967, the overall growth rate of such movements has overtaken the expansion rate of the Catholic and Protestant churches in at least sixteen African countries (Barrett 1968: 3, 34, 72). E. G. Parrinder notes that these autonomous expressions of African Christianity represent the fastest and most effective way of spreading Christianity in Africa.

James Fernandez suggested in 1979 that this growth process is continuing, indicating that "there has indeed been a prodigious growth and spread of religious movements in Africa. Present conservative estimates place membership in the diverse contemporary religious groups at well over 10 million. There may be as many as 10 thousand different movements. Numbers alone command our attention" (p. xvii). Although it is impossible to determine in precise statistics how much of the religious life of Africa these movements represent, their magnitude is nonetheless apparent.

The Harrist movement developed during the end of the nineteenth century and the beginning of the twentieth, when other important Christianity-inspired religious movements were arising in West Africa.[3] When Harris arrived in the Ivory Coast, the French were completing their consolidation of control over the populations of the new colony. In the previous sixty-five years, the coastal Ivorian societies had experienced important alterations in their relations with the Europeans, changes that had significantly affected the Africans' social structures and belief systems.

West Africans had once welcomed the Europeans, and trade with various European nations brought some Africans new goods and increased prosperity. When the French sought to reduce the commercial role of the Ivorians in the coastal trade in order to increase their own control and profits, however, the Ivorians retaliated with hostilities against them. The French induced local chiefs to sign treaties, which the Africans had hoped would allow them to maintain sovereignty and would prove beneficial to themselves. But in addition to declaring the colonial status of the Ivory Coast territory, the French made increasing numbers of demands on the Ivorians, to which they were forced to submit because of the superior military force of the French.

Responding to the intrusion, village chiefs led their people in revolts against the French occupation, and village priests called on the traditional spirits to help them overcome the intruders. Both efforts were unsuccessful. From a position of relative commercial equality with the Europeans, the Ivorians found themselves economically and politically dominated by the French. The culmination of the French thrust to gain total control of the colony by force was in full swing when the Prophet Harris arrived.

He came offering to the Ivorians a new religion, one better able than the indigenous system to explain and provide methods for coping with the problems that resulted from the colonial situation. Although he preached a doctrine similar to that of the missionaries, Harris's message was adapted to the understanding and needs of his audience. Because he was an African from a traditional background who could also interact effectively in the western milieu, Harris was culturally appropriate to the task of bringing to the Ivorians a new religious orientation and a gospel of liberation that was a synthesis of old and new.

On the basis of his own understanding of Christianity and his commitment to his mission, the Prophet Harris offered to the Ivorians a new program of his own creation, which struck a responsive chord. Articulating the confusion and desires of his followers, he also created new desires among them by showing them what was possible both within their own societies and in their interaction with Europeans. He offered them a very welcome message of hope that they might end the oppressive colonial situation. All they had to do was to listen to his teachings, heed his instructions, and follow his example. Harris's message to the Ivorians provided them with a new way of understanding their present life situation, as well as the means of improving it.

Harris set out to convert people to Christianity. He left the details of the content of this Christianity to others: to foreign missionaries and to the Ivorians themselves, many of whom rejected the missionary institutions to create an institution of their own.

The origins of both the Harrist movement and the Harrist church distinguish themselves as unique among similar phenomena in Africa. Barrett characterizes the Harrist movement as the "most remarkable of all indigenous movements to Christianity in West Africa." Noting that few Christian movements have been founded de novo by African leaders and prophets, with no foreign assistance, and not originating out of a separation from a mission church, he portrays the Harrist movement as the classic case of this type of phenomenon.[4]

Indeed, Harris did not lead a discontented flock in separating from a missionary church, as in the case of many such movements. On the contrary, he undertook to Christianize a population with whom the missionaries had had almost no success; and rather than leading them away from the missionary churches, he sent his converts to them. The prophet's role and example are unique because he is the only individual in the religious history of the African continent to have led such a multitude of Africans to Christianity. That he did so in a matter of months, under extremely difficult circumstances, makes his phenomenal success even more impressive.

The creation of the Harrist church, like the prophetic movement out of which it grew, represents a further evolution of the manifestation of indigenous initiative of which Harris was an example and a symbol. Like the Harrist movement, the Harrist church differed markedly from the more common separatist phenomena having their origin in the messages of European missionaries. Harrists built churches and worshiped according to the prophet's teachings, independently of the Catholic churches present, and prior to the arrival of the Protestant missionaries. The Harrist church institutionalized the Prophet Harris's message. Ivorians learned to be Christians from a Liberian prophet who himself had been converted to Christianity by an African.

PART 1

The Harrist Movement

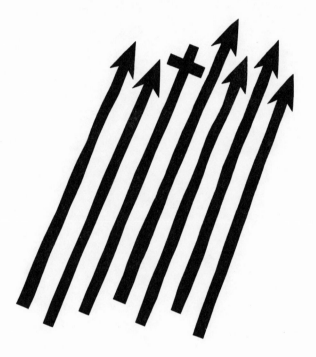

CHAPTER 1

The West African Reformer

Liberia: The Great Black Hope

It is of especial significance that the Harrist church was inspired by the vision of a native Liberian prophet. Liberia was an uncommon country in Africa. Its creation was inspired by the dynamics of race relations in the United States and by the dreams of freedom of Afro-Americans whose ancestors had been brutally torn from their homelands during the slave trade. Many Afro-Americans longed to return to Africa, believing that there they could find the freedom they had never experienced in the United States. Groups of slaves had petitioned for their freedom prior to the Revolutionary War, indicating their desire to return to Africa, and in 1815 Paul Cuffee, at his own expense, transported thirty-eight Afro-Americans to Sierra Leone (J. Harris 1972: 87–88).

Slaveholders, politicians, and other members of the white establishment also began to view Afro-American immigration to Africa as a solution to what they saw as the problem of the free blacks. The presence of free Afro-Americans in the slave states was seen as a threat to the institution of slavery, providing proof that black people were not born to be slaves, as most whites maintained. Additionally, free black people also aided slaves and organized resistance to the system. The American Colonization Society was developed to repatriate these free blacks to Africa, and Liberia was born in 1821 when the first group of Afro-American settlers set foot on ancestral soil (J. Harris 1972: 88–89).

The State of Maryland was a leader in the repatriation scheme because it had, in 1830, the largest free black community in the South. Frightened by the Nat Turner slave revolt in neighboring

3

Virginia, Maryland in 1831 adopted a program directed toward repatriating all free blacks from the state to Africa. An estimated 70 percent of Maryland's manumitted blacks returned to Africa— hence the creation of Maryland County, Liberia (Hill and Kilson 1971: 37–38). Whereas many whites were anxious to rid themselves of free blacks by sending them to Africa, those Afro-Americans who chose to immigrate to Liberia did so gladly in the anticipation of a better life. Numbers of idealistic Afro-American leaders settled in Liberia, or worked there for extended periods of time, and urged other Afro-Americans to join them there.

Such Afro-American leaders as Edward Wilmot Blyden, Alexander Crummell, and the Honorable John Henry Smyth helped to shape the intellectual climate of nineteenth-century Liberia. These men's personal experiences and the group experience of people of African origin in the Americas convinced them that Afro-Americans could not become free and equal human beings in a racist society that thrived on human exploitation and slavery. They maintained that Afro-Americans had an obligation to themselves and to the descendants of their own African ancestors remaining on the continent. With the knowledge acquired during their intimate involvement with western society, they hoped to redeem Africa from continued European and American exploitation and from its depressed state of material and technological development. Paul Cuffee's statement is revelatory of this perspective: "As I am of the African race, I feel myself interested for them, and, if I am favored with a talent, I think I am willing that they should be benefitted thereby" (S. Harris 1972: 39). Pro-immigration Afro-American leaders believed that only on the African continent could Afro-Americans find true freedom and independence. They also believed that their creation of an independent republic in Africa would demonstrate the Afro-American capacity for self-rule, and contribute to the ending of slavery in the United States.

The goal of the resettlement of formerly enslaved Afro-Americans in Liberia is well expressed by Lott Carey in his personal statement about the United States: "I am an African, and in this country, however meritorious my conduct and respectable my character, I cannot receive the credit due to either. I wish to go to a country where I shall be esteemed by my merits, not by my complexion, and I feel bound to labor for my suffering race." An ex-slave who had saved his money and bought his freedom, Carey worked as a physician in Sierra Leone and went to Liberia in 1821 as one of the first two Afro-American missionaries. Later he was appointed acting governor of Liberia (Hill and Kilson 1971: 90).

The best-known and most influential of the Afro-American leaders in Liberia was Edward Wilmot Blyden, a native of St. Thomas who, having met with racial discrimination when he wished to go to school in the United States, finished his education in Liberia where he became a statesman, diplomat, orator, educator, and prolific writer. Blyden was the exponent of ideas that circulated widely along the West Coast of Africa. He edited and wrote articles for, and his speeches were reproduced in, the newspapers that were carried by steamer to the English-speaking coastal cities from Freetown, Sierra Leone, to Lagos, Nigeria (Livingston 1975; Lynch 1967).

Believing that, with the help of the western knowledge brought back to the continent by the Afro-Americans, Liberia was destined to redeem all persons of African ancestry, Blyden accepted the challenge of proving that black people could manage their own affairs. In many of his speeches in Africa and abroad, Blyden advocated a synthesis of African and western cultures. While president of Liberia College, he worked to develop it into an institution oriented both to African culture and to western learning. He called Afro-Americans to return from the United States, Canada, and the West Indies in order to participate in this cultural symbiosis, saying, "Liberia with its outstretched arms invites all to come" (J. Harris 1972: 92).

Blyden was favorably disposed to many facets of indigenous African life. In his book *African Life and Customs* (1908), he championed polygamy, communalism, and indigenous African religious forms, insisting that Africans should continue to learn the knowledge of their ancestors. He was pleased when native African students began to attend Liberia College, and he hoped that, in addition to learning western knowledge and skills in school, they would also retain the best of their own cultural heritage. They could then return to their people to act as modernizing agents, without having been estranged from them by the acquisition of foreign knowledge, tastes, and habits (Livingston 1975: 45, 124).[1]

In 1891, in Lagos, Nigeria, Blyden made a speech entitled "The

Return of Exiles and the West African Church," in which he said that as long as the evangelization of Africa was left in foreign hands and imposed through alien forms, it would never be accomplished (Webster 1964: 65). He was an outspoken critic of Christian missionaries because of the Euro-American churches' roles both in contributing to the perpetuation of slavery in the Americas and in trying to destroy indigenous institutions in Africa. Blyden asserted the need for an autonomous African church, distinct from and undivided by the denominationalism of the missionary churches. In this church, Africans would be free to develop according to their own traditions and inclinations, rather than being forced to try to conform to white norms and styles (Livingston 1975: 46, 84, 99).

Blyden's sentiments concerning Euro-American Christianity were echoed by John Henry Smyth, who served from 1879 to 1883 as U.S. minister to Liberia:

> The ships which brought priests as outward passengers took the human product of the race back as homeward cargo. . . . The fetich of the cross in the hands of the Portuguese, did not deter them from knavery and theft and murder, and the Congoes concluded that their fetiches were less harmful than the alien Portuguese. . . . Alien races can aid the progress of Christianity and civilization among Africans, but cannot control it with the hope of ultimate success in Africa. [Smyth 1896/1971: 63]

Historian Joseph E. Harris concurs with the opinions of men like Blyden and Smyth concerning the effects of the Euro-American missionary efforts, which he characterizes as "this European initiative, emanating from people whose cultures historically demeaned things African":

> With an unquestioned belief in their own self-righteousness and the depravity of Africans, missionaries were determined to change indigenous institutions and behavior and thus saw themselves as Christian agents of civilization. This conclusion meant that Africans had to be taught different values, goals, and modes of behavior. Consequently, missionary schools became the keystone of the missions' activities. The curricula of those schools either ignored or distorted African culture and emphasized European history and culture, thereby instilling the idea that the

important developments of the past, even for Africans, occurred in Europe. It was only with the greatest of perseverance, therefore, that mission-trained Africans retained a sense of pride and confidence in their heritage and people, and a commitment to African freedom.

Missionaries, quite naturally, tended to identify with the colonial officials, with whom they shared nationality, culture, general way of life, and on whom they frequently relied for protection and contact with the outside world. In this sense, and to the extent that mission schools supplied clerks, interpreters, and others for the government, missionaries often became allies of the colonial administrations.

Missionaries established hospitals, clinics, health centers, refugee camps; they studied and provided curative and preventive medicines for tropical diseases; they studied and supplied a script for several African languages; they encouraged the development of legitimate trade to replace the slave trade; and a few of them provided useful accounts of African life. It should be stressed, however, that African assistants contributed to each of these endeavors, though they receive little credit in the records.

Had the missionaries not gone to Africa as a censor, not sought a deliberate destruction of African values and customs, not attempted to teach the worthlessness of the African past, not supported white superiority, all of their contributions would have had greater meaning and would have led to more positive race relations. As it turned out, however, from about the last decade of the nineteenth century, some mission-trained Africans began to demand greater religious responsibilities for themselves, a greater respect for African culture (music, dance, language, beliefs, customs), and racial equality. These concerns launched the independent church movements whose objective was to develop separate African churches that would be Christian while identifying with African cultural and physical needs. [J. Harris 1972: 180–81]

Afro-American leaders in Liberia were also aware of Liberia's political and economic importance for Europe, and of the meaning of these factors for both Afro-Americans and native Africans. Alexander Crummell, an Episcopal priest who was the grandson of a Temne chief from Sierra Leone, spent twenty years working in West Africa. Author of *The Future of Africa* (1862), a 354-page collection of sermons and addresses pronounced in Liberia, and of *Africa and America* (1891), Crummell in 1860 wrote a letter to a friend in New York entitled "The Relations and Duties of Free Colored Men in America to Africa." In his letter he talked about the rich natural treasures of the continent as God's gift to the children of Africa, and lamented, "Now all of this flows into the coffers of the white men. . . . the larger advantages of it go to Europe and America, and help to swell the broad stream of their wealth, luxury, and refinement." In suggesting that free Afro-Americans begin to follow the example of whites in investing funds and skills to help develop the resources of the continent, Crummell intended the beneficiaries to be all of Africa's children at home and abroad (Hill and Kilson 1971: 99–102).

Detailing specific ways in which Afro-Americans might involve themselves in the development of the African continent, in turn helping themselves, Crummell described the material advantages Afro-Americans could acquire by beginning large-scale trade enterprises with the West African coast. He went on to say, "These are some of the material influences which would result . . . the moral and philanthropic results would be equally if not more notable. The kings and tradesmen of Africa, having the demonstration of Negro capacity before them, would hail the presence of the Black kinsmen from America, and would be stimulated to a generous emulation" (Crummell 1861/1971: 103–4).

In 1882, as U.S. minister to Liberia, John Henry Smyth sent a dispatch to the United States concerning England's desire to annex part of the territory of the independent nation of Liberia, under the pretext that the indigenous Africans were displeased with the control of the Liberian government. Understanding that England was interested in involving itself with the concerns of the Africans only "where such interference is most likely to be followed by material benefits to England," Smyth wrote:

> In this particular instance, it is indubitable that if Liberia be ousted of her possession and right, the aboriginal races [of] the territory will become vassals and the land, the property of her majesty's colonial government of Sierra Leone, and the rich oil

and forest possessions will be guarded and protected for the enrichment of England with little reference to whether the Negro is benefitted or not. While there can be no doubt from West African precedent but that England will, should she take this territory . . . afford more immediate and ample facilities for cultivation among the native races of Western civilization than Liberia can now afford, yet she is likely to make the Negroes here subservient to her too frequently incompetent and unsympathetic British representative traders, and thereby destroy that self-dependence that heathen and barbarous races must in a measure retain in taking upon themselves alien civilizations, if they are to amount to anything more than a servile and an imitative class. In other words, the benefits of such control will be on the side of the civilizer, England, and the civilized will possess doubtful good, questionable advantage. With nations as with individuals, elevation should be from within—by growth, not from without—by mounting upon others. [Smyth 1882/1971: 109–110]

Liberia's political and economic well-being was fraught with problems stemming from the external pressures of the European powers on the independent black nation. Liberia suffered insults and aggression at the hands of the colonial powers, and during the 1880s was prevented from trading with its African neighbors who were under British and French domination (J. Harris 1972: 90). The Afro-American settlers, however, worked hard at the tasks of developing and unifying the country. According to Joseph E. Harris:

That their progress was slow was due not only to their cultural difference from the masses, but also to powerful, unsympathetic, and sometimes conniving Europeans and Americans who sought to isolate and stunt Liberia's development.

Still, with independence [which the settlers had declared in 1847], Liberia became a unique phenomenon in Africa. Not only did it result from the repatriation of Africans from abroad, it became the only internationally recognized independent African country, except Ethiopia, until well into the twentieth century. But precisely because of its unique status and history, *Liberia became a symbol of hope for the regeneration of Africans at home and abroad*. The Liberian Declaration of Independence noted that the Liberians had been inhabitants of the United States where they were debarred from all the rights and privileges of human beings. Their coming to Africa, therefore, represented to them an opportunity to exercise their freedom, and within a few years, *Liberian leaders envisioned their country as destined to become a province of freedom for the uplift of all persons of African descent.* [1972: 91; emphasis added]

The Grebo, the Government, and the Church

William Wade Harris was a member of the Grebo ethnic group located in Maryland County in the southeastern coastal area of Liberia, bordering on the Ivory Coast.[2] The Grebo are part of the larger Kru-speaking language family who live on both sides of the Cavalla River, which separates Liberia from the Ivory Coast. Treaties drawn up between the Grebo and the Afro-American settlers living in Maryland County stipulated that the settlers would provide free schools and churches to be attended by both Africans and settlers, and would teach the Grebo the advantages of their lifestyle. In return, the settlers would be allowed to purchase land and would be assisted by the Grebo in adapting to the new environment.

Unfortunately, cultural differences between the two groups took a toll. The settlers disapproved of aspects of Grebo culture; and many Grebo regretted selling their land and allowing the settlers to interfere with their lives. Incidents broke out between the two groups, culminating in a series of "Grebo Wars" between 1857 and 1910. The Grebo refused to acknowledge the Liberian government's sovereignty over them because, they insisted, the settlers had not fulfilled their side of the treaties, and because measures taken by the settler government in its own interest were seen by the Grebo as detrimental to their own welfare. As a result of the wars, new treaties were established, settling land disputes and guaranteeing equal rights to the indigenous populations.

In spite of their animosity toward the Liberian government, which had usurped their sovereignty in creating the nation, the Grebo were intensively exposed to the settlers' life-style beginning in 1834; they learned new techniques as they helped the newcomers get established. They assisted the settlers in building stone and wooden houses, and having learned such skills as carpentry and brickmasonry from them, began building their own houses in the same fashion. They also acquired from the settlers new tastes in food, clothing, and household furnishings, and a Grebo elite developed that associated closely with the new Americo-Liberians. Grebo families sometimes sent their children to live with settler families to get the benefit of a western education and life-style in exchange for household work (Haliburton 1971: 7–10).

Initially, the repatriated Afro-Americans dominated positions in business, education, government, and the churches. By means of the educational system, however, the government soon began to assimilate the indigenous Africans, who were far more numerous than the settlers, into all levels of life. The school population became overwhelmingly African, and by the early twentieth century, the indigenous ethnic groups, including the Grebo, were represented in high governmental positions (Harris 1972: 90–91).

Methodist and Episcopal missionaries accompanied the Afro-American settlers to Liberia. The Methodist church oriented its efforts mainly toward the settlers, although some Grebo also became members. The Episcopal church interested itself mainly in converting the African populations. Episcopal missionaries learned the Grebo language, devised a system of notation for it, and, starting in 1839, published a Grebo-English dictionary and four hundred hymns and part of the gospels and prayer books in the language, as well as holding church services in Grebo. Putting great stress on providing schools for both children and adults, the Episcopalians taught many Grebo to read and write their own language, as well as some English. The Episcopalians also emphasized the training of native clergy and in 1865 ordained their first two Grebo ministers— S. W. Kla Seton and M. P. Keda Valentine—both of whom added Euro-American surnames to their Grebo names as indications of their new status.[3]

Although the history of the Christianization of Africa has been written as if it had been accomplished by European missionaries, in reality African ministers did most of the work of spreading Christianity on the continent (Cason 1962: 150; Haliburton 1971: 11–14; Republic of Liberia Interior Department 1957: 172; F. Walker 1927a: 136). In Liberia, Christian converts acted as lay evangelists. Convinced of the power of their new god, they would seek occasions to pit it against the power of the indigenous spirits, challenging traditional priests. According to an account of one such occurrence, a Grebo evangelist named Gnebevi was teaching Sunday school in a village in which a traditional priest was being inducted into office. To test the power of the Christian god, Gnebevi and his congregation prayed that the priest might be embarrassed. When the priest was unable to perform one of the feats required of him, the Christians present were convinced of the superior power of their god (Cason 1962: 152–53).

The church services of the Protestant missionaries were very emotional affairs, the ministers insisting that they were preaching the true Word of God as contained in the Bible. The ministers' fiery exhortations urged sinners to repent from mortal sin. Ministers told their listeners to stop worshiping their indigenous spirits and observing the religious practices of their own people, and to worship the missionaries' god instead. Other "un-Christian" behavior included the drinking of alcohol, failure to respect the Sabbath, and especially the practice of polygamy, which the missionaries considered most immoral. Foreign missionaries in Africa waged an all-out war on the fundamental social institution of polygamy as if formal monogamy were a prerequisite for Christianity, not just for membership in Western society.[4] The missionaries measured people's conversion from the traditional religion to Christianity by their destruction of the altars and other material artifacts representing their indigenous spirits.

The Making of a Prophet

Who was the man who almost single-handedly, in a matter of months, revolutionized the religious life of almost the entire southern Ivory Coast? William Wade (pronounced, and alternatively spelled, "Waddy") Harris was born between 1850 and 1865[5] in the village of Graway near Cape Palmas, close to the Ivory Coast border, of nonliterate, non-Christianized parents. Wade is a common Grebo name, and many Christianized Grebo, like the first two ordained Episcopal ministers, added European surnames to their Grebo names.[6] It is probable that Harris assumed this name as a young adult, perhaps in connection with his religious conversion or his evolving professional responsibilities.

Harris's childhood was apparently that of an average Grebo boy. At the age of twelve, however, he was sent by his parents to live with the Reverend Jesse Lowrie, a Grebo minister active in the American Methodist Episcopal Mission, who presided over the mission school in nearby Sinoe. While living with Lowrie, young Wade attended school, where he learned to read and write in Grebo and English and was baptized as a Methodist. He was also exposed to the amenities of the settler life-style adopted by many Grebo Methodists (Haliburton 1971: 9–12).

After a few years, Wade, true to the tradition of young unmarried Grebo men, took a job with the crew[7] of one of the British merchant ships that traveled along the African coast, stopping in different countries. During such travels, he had the opportunity to observe and compare the various ways in which other Africans lived. While he was in Lagos, Nigeria, he attended the Tinubu Wesleyan church, one of the separatist "African churches" being developed at the time by the members of the Nigerian elite who wished to be both Christian and free of foreign missionary influences (Haliburton 1971: 13; Webster 1964: 109).

Having accumulated enough money to begin a family, Wade returned to Liberia and began to work as a brickmason. At the age of twenty-one, he joined the American Methodist church at Cape Palmas. After his faith was aroused by a second Liberian minister, Reverend Thompson, Harris became an active lay minister. He married Rose Badick Farr, with whom he had six children (Haliburton 1971: 13).

After a few years, Harris left the Methodist church and was confirmed as a member of the Episcopal church. This change may have reflected the evolution of his political consciousness, in view of the Episcopal mission's orientation toward Grebo rather than settler culture. He became a lay preacher in the Episcopal church and preached the same message as the American missionaries: the need to give up indigenous beliefs and practices and to worship only the Christian god.

As evidence of Harris's Christian fervor, Gordon Haliburton cites an occasion on which he risked his life to rescue a man accused of witchcraft from being subjected to the sasswood ordeal.[8] A year later, however, when Harris was involved in a political struggle in Graway, he is said to have accused his enemies of practicing witchcraft (Haliburton 1971: 13–16). His fervor as a Christian preacher thus did not preclude a continued belief in the efficacy of certain traditional practices.

Harris left his job as a brickmason to become an assistant school-teacher at the American Protestant Episcopal mission in Half Graway in 1892. In this position he taught reading and writing for ten years. He was then put in charge of the Spring Hill school in Graway. Later he took charge of a boarding school in Half Graway, where he was responsible for sixteen pupils. In addition, he acquired the influential position of government interpreter (Haliburton 1971: 14–15).

While he was working as a government interpreter, Harris was charged with the task of acting as a peacemaker between two hostile factions in the Graway area. Instead of trying to end the hostilities, however, Harris led an opposition group against the paramount chief of Graway, whom he believed to be too dutiful a servant of the Liberian government. The government tried to restore the chief by gaining the assistance of another senior chief, but Harris triumphed by mobilizing the local people and threatening to put the deposed chief's rival in office with their support (Haliburton 1971: 16).

The Liberian authorities called Harris to Monrovia to account for his disloyalty. When he failed to appear, he was dismissed from his position as government interpreter. In response, he wrote angry letters to the bishop and superintendent of Maryland County, referring to himself as the "Secretary of the Graway People" (Haliburton 1971: 16).

Harris then went to Monrovia to complain about his dismissal. He called on the state treasurer and on President Arthur Barclay. Receiving no satisfaction, Harris apparently returned home in a very emotional state. Rebuked for going barefoot, conduct incompatible with his role as teacher and evangelist, he is said to have responded, "When you see me again you will see me with a big cloth on. . . . Look here, I am going back into heathenism. I am going to take off all these clothes" (Haliburton 1971: 30).

During this period, the beginning of 1909, the Liberian government suspected that a plot was underway to provoke a coup d'état. Harris, who like many Grebo was discontented with the government, was suspected of being one of the leaders involved in the

alleged plot. On 11 or 13 February 1909, Harris performed the act
that earned him the nickname "Old Pa Union Jack" from some of
his chroniclers. With a band of followers he lowered the Liberian
flag and raised the British flag in its place on Paduke Beach near
Harper, while his supporters shouted insults at America-Liberian
onlookers. He was arrested, convicted of treason, and imprisoned
for more than a year (Haliburton 1971: 30–31).

In prison he spent a good deal of time praying and reading the
Bible. One day, while praying, he had a vision of the Angel Gabriel
telling him that he had been chosen by God to preach his Word to
all people who had not yet heard the Christian message. According
to the description of the event Harris gave to a Protestant missionary, Gabriel told him that his role was to be like that of the
prophets of the Bible, "like Elijah who burned all the priests of
Baal." He was told, "Go and teach all nations, baptizing them. . . .
So I go and baptize" (Platt 1934: 53).

Upon his release from prison, Harris began wearing a long white
robe with a long black scarf around his neck, and a small round
white hat. One report said that the style of his dress was dictated in
his vision (F. Walker 1927a: 141), but Parrinder suggests that the
costume may have been inspired by Islamic Hausas Harris had seen
in Nigeria (1969: 151). Bishop Henry McNeal Turner noted in a
letter written from West Africa in 1918 that "all of the missionaries
here . . . wear robes" (Turner 1893/1971: 267); perhaps Harris was
merely dressing in keeping with his milieu.

Harris tried unsuccessfully to pursue his divine calling in Liberia;
just as the masses had ridiculed the prophets of other lands in other
times, the Liberians also scorned their prophet. Some people who
knew him before his imprisonment simply assumed that he had
been deranged by his prison experience.

In 1913, determined to pursue his mission, Harris headed east to
the Ivory Coast with two female companions (his wife had died
before his departure). One woman was a villager who later bore the
prophet's child. The other was probably the educated widow of
M. P. Keda Valentine (one of the first Grebo Episcopal priests), who
had had a vision telling her to accompany Harris (Haliburton 1971:
141).

Harris explained the nature of his mission to Father Hartz, director of the Catholic missions in the Ivory Coast, in what Hartz characterized as the "pure and correct English for which Great Britain takes pride." The explanation was this:

> I am a Prophet; above all religions and not subject to the control of men. I am only responsible to God through the intermediary of the Angel Gabriel. . . . [Gabriel said to me] I will accompany you everywhere and will reveal to you the mission for which God, the Master of the Universe Whom men no longer respect, has chosen you. . . . [Gabriel] initiates me bit by bit into my mission as Prophet of modern times, of the Era of Peace, of which St. John speaks in the twentieth chapter of the Apocalypse, and of which the coming is near. I must lead the lost nations back to Christ, and for that I must threaten them with the most fearful punishment in order that they will allow themselves to be baptized and instructed by the Catholic and Protestant men of God. I must make the cult of the Natural Law and the divine precepts reign here, especially the observance of the Sabbath which is so little respected. I have come to speak to all of the people, black and white, of this country. No excessive drinking of alcohol. Respect for authority. I tolerate polygamy, but I prohibit adultery. The thunder will speak, the angels will punish the world if people do not listen to my words, the words of God interpreted for you. I am sent by Christ, and I must without fail fulfill the deeds and gestures that He inspires in me. I go across the land pushed by the breath from Above. I speak only with the inspiration from heaven. [van Bulck 1961: 121–22]

Harris's mission was a phenomenal success in the Ivory Coast and the southwestern corner of the Gold Coast (now Ghana). In 1914, precisely because he was so successful, the French colonial administration expelled him from the Ivory Coast. The prophet attempted on several occasions to return from Liberia to the Ivory Coast to pursue his mission, but was stopped each time by French border guards. He traveled to Sierra Leone in 1917, but failed to have the appeal there that he had had in the Ivory Coast.

Until his death in 1929, Harris traveled around Liberia on preaching tours. According to an early chronicler, the prophet baptized five hundred people on one occasion. Traditionally oriented Africans respected him, considering him a true messenger of God.

Many of the settlers and the African elite, however, labeled him a simpleminded fanatic (Amos-Djoro 1956: 200; F. Walker 1927a: 141). According to Protestant missionary Pierre Benoit, who visited the prophet in 1926, no missions in Liberia acknowledged the work that Harris was doing. He would preach to, convert, and baptize people and then direct them to the Protestant missions, where they would be rebaptized (Platt 1934: 57).

The Prophet's Inspiration

What was it about the background and personality of William Wade Harris that allowed him to undertake successfully the mission of converting tens of thousands of Africans to Christianity? His work on the British ships along the coast while he was an adolescent had permitted him to visit different countries, to encounter a variety of Africans and whites, and to acquire a broad range of experiences to which most Africans were not exposed. The combination of a traditional childhood and several adolescent years with a fellow Grebo whose life-style was like that of the settlers allowed Harris a familiarity with both cultures. Literate in both English and Grebo, he also had the educational background necessary for a number of leadership roles.

In his positions as teacher, school director, lay preacher, and government interpreter, Harris also served as cultural mediator. As teacher and preacher, he taught elements of western culture to his own people; and as a government interpreter, in addition to translating the languages, he was called upon to interpret elements of African culture to the settlers and vice versa. The Liberian government manifested recognition of his talent as a cultural mediator by enlisting his assistance as peacemaker during the turmoil in Graway, and its apprehension of him as a possible rebel leader is an indication of his ability to convince and mobilize people. That he was committed to his principles and had the courage of his convictions is evidenced by the Union Jack episode. That he also saw himself as a leader of people is clear in his references to himself as the "Secretary of the Graway people" in his letters to the county government.

Harris's leadership qualities, then, were well recognized in different quarters, and he seems to have benefited from the corresponding prestige. He was able, after his dismissal from his job as interpreter, to call not only upon the state treasurer, but also upon the president of the country—seemingly not a small feat for a simple "Kru-boy," as he referred to himself in marveling to Protestant missionary Pierre Benoit that he should have accomplished such an amazing mission in the Ivory Coast.

William Wade Harris does not emerge as a simpleminded, primitive charlatan who confused his dreams with reality, as some early writers characterized him.[9] He comes forth, rather, as an intelligent and influential social and political leader—a man who used his broad experience to try to educate his fellow Africans and who urged them to try to change their society in ways that he, and many of them, considered to be in their best interests.

Harris had been an active and zealous evangelist, and joining the Methodist church may have been his initial step toward becoming a prophet. He told Benoit in 1926: "I was first converted here, at Cape Palmas, when the minister preached in the church on Revelations 2:4, 5: 'That which I have against you is that you have abandoned your first love; turn then from whence you have fallen; repent and do your former works. . . .' The same year I began to preach. I felt the Holy Spirit come upon me and change me at the moment of my conversion in the church."[10]

That the vision of the Angel Gabriel informing him of his mission was not an abrupt delusion, discontinuous with his past life, is indicated by a statement he made in the Ivory Coast to Father Hartz: "Wesleyan teacher and preacher when the pastor is absent, I prepare myself for my role of prophet through prayer, reading and studying the Bible. The Angel instructs me about the times to come; . . . [about] the ruses of the great dragon . . . who will be enchained for a thousand years" (van Bulck 1961: 122).

The Last Prophet

Excluding for the sake of more mundane explanations the possibility that the Angel Gabriel really did communicate God's will to Harris on several occasions, how can one account for Harris's prison experience and subsequent commitment to fulfilling what he believed to be his divine responsibility? In view of Harris's background as an educator, lay religious leader, and political activist, how did he become a prophet, delegated by the Christian god with the mission of bringing his Word to the unconverted in order to save them, lest they lead themselves to perdition through their evil practices?

The catalyst that triggered and provided the stage for Harris's transformation was situational. Harris was a member of a select company of individuals—each in his or her own historical time and place—who have received spiritual revelations during a period of confinement. All such revelations do not involve visions of heavenly figures, of course, and few of the individuals become prophets, but a number of them have become leaders.

If Harris really felt, prior to his vision, that he was consciously preparing himself for a greater role as a religious leader, he might reasonably have interpreted the period in prison as an opportunity to increase his biblical knowledge, and possibly he saw it as a trial period marking the turning point in his life. If he had not previously aspired to become a great religious leader, his reading of the Bible, particularly the texts about the Christian prophets, would appear to have convinced him that he had the proper preparation and qualities for the role. Reflecting back over his life with the broad perspective of his advanced age, with the awareness that as a lay preacher he had successfully converted many people from their old beliefs to Christianity, Harris realized that this was exactly what the biblical prophets with whom he began to compare himself had done.

In describing the circumstances of his initial call, he told Benoit that Gabriel had said to him: "You are not in prison. God is coming to anoint you. You will be a prophet. Your case resembles that of Shadrach, Meshack, and Abednego; you are like Daniel" (Haliburton 1971: 35). Asked by Benoit how he knew that the vision was real, he replied: "It is like Hebrews 9:1. Faith is a firm assurance in the things one hopes for; a revelation of those things which are never seen. You do not see these things, but they possess you." Asked whence came his authority, he cited Matt. 28:19: "Go and teach all nations, baptizing them. . . ." Asked what he was commissioned to do, he said: "I am like the watchman, like Ezekial 33. I Cry, 'Prepare ye, prepare ye.' The Spirit of God speaks to me through the Bible and teaches us all these things" (Platt 1934: 51–52). When he was released from prison he went about preaching,

"Prepare ye, prepare ye, Jesus Christ is at hand. Repent ye. I say to all men, black or white, to repent and believe in Jesus Christ. I am his last prophet" (Haliburton 971: 35).

Missionaries questioned Harris's knowledge of the Bible, assuming it to be very meager, but Benoit made note of the prophet's remarkable knowledge of the Bible: "In it he searches for explanations, examples, and proofs to support all he says. He can adapt wonderfully some situation or some attitude of his adversary to a text, and find an analogy in the Scriptures" (F. Walker 1927a: 140).

Thus, the Prophet Harris emerges as a man who had deep Christian religious convictions throughout his adult life, as well as an extensive knowledge of the Bible. His lay preaching against the worship of indigenous spirits and in favor of Christian beliefs foreshadowed his activities in the Ivory Coast.

It is significant that Harris was taught Christianity, not by foreign missionaries from a different cultural tradition, but by members of his own ethnic group, who were first-generation African Christian ministers who understood Christianity within the conceptual framework of their own culture and with whom he shared certain fundamental assumptions. Unlike the foreign missionaries, these Liberian ministers acknowledged the reality and efficacy of the indigenous spiritual forces, although they had become committed to Christianity as a superior religious system. That Harris accused someone of practicing witchcraft, for example, does not indicate that he was not a good Christian. He had seen what were defined as results of witchcraft in his daily life and thus had no reason to question its reality. He was, on the contrary, a good Christian in that he urged people to cease practicing witchcraft not only because it was reprehensible in the indigenous system, but also, and more importantly, because it was contrary to Christian morality.

Furthermore, the Liberians from whom Harris learned about Christianity were less likely than the foreign missionaries to be so vehement about suppressing aspects of social behavior that the missionaries defined as "un-Christian"—meaning un-Western—that the Africans understood to be fundamental to their way of life. Coming from a context in which the pattern of Africans' teaching Christianity to Africans was common, the Prophet Harris learned Christianity, and could present it, in a culturally mediated form, true to the Bible and yet adapted to the understanding and concerns of an African audience. Accordingly, he was able to superimpose Christianity upon an indigenous religious substratum in the firm belief that Christianity was the superior force.

In doing so, Harris was actually putting into practice the idea of Blyden and other Afro-American proponents of Afro-American repatriation that the Africans should maintain their own institutions and values while learning aspects of European and American culture. Harris exemplified Blyden's ideal of an African who had acquired western knowledge without becoming estranged from his own culture, and who therefore could teach this new knowledge to his people in a manner meaningful and acceptable to them. In fact, Harris's career consistently embodied key elements of Blyden's philosophy and ideals. Because of Blyden's prominence in Liberia, Harris must have been familiar with his ideas.[11] Indeed, Haliburton suggests both that Harris may have been directly influenced by Blyden's ideas in the style of his prophetic activities and that the Union Jack incident may actually have been part of a coup d'état attempt in which Blyden himself may have been involved (1971: 30–31).

Thus, in pursuing his divinely ordained mission of conversion among the populations of the Ivory Coast, and in sowing the seeds for the creation of a new African religious institution, the Prophet Harris became a part of the larger process of the realization of the dreams of those Afro-American leaders who returned home to Africa to work toward the redemption of all people of African descent. Charged with the task of showing the path of spiritual salvation to the lost nations and bringing them back to the worship of the universal creator god, Harris also offered his fellow Africans a message of more secular salvation from the oppressive ravages of the colonial system to which the creator god's unfortunate African children had fallen prey.

CHAPTER 2

The Ivory Coast before Harris

Life on the Lagoons

In order for the Prophet Harris's mission to be successful, the new conceptual scheme and forms of religious and social organization about which he taught had to strike responsive chords in the sociocultural milieu of his audience. The content and form of the prophet's message and his manner of presentation fit especially well into the religious system of the peoples living in the lagoons area of the country where Harris spent the most time.[1] It was in this area, at the center of the powerful French colonial administration, that Harris had his greatest influence, and it is there that the Harrist churches are now concentrated.

The ethnic groups of the lagoons area are the Avikam or Brignan, Alladian, Adjoukrou, Abidji, Attié, Abbey, Ebrié, and other smaller groups.[2] Although there are some significant differences among these ethnic groups, they share similar fishing and agricultural lifestyles as well as many social and cultural traits—such as similar religious systems and age-grade structures—which have been accentuated by cultural diffusion and by intermarriage. People from one ethnic group have been absorbed into another, and some groups are conscious of having acquired certain specific institutions from others.

VILLAGE ORGANIZATION

Of the lagoons ethnic groups, it was the Ebrié with whom Harris had the most extensive and intimate contact and on whose lives he had the most direct and lasting impact. The Ebrié

22

presently constitute the majority of the membership and leadership of the Harrist church. Among the Ebrié, village political, cultural, and religious life is organized in accordance with the age-grade structure. Among the lagoons ethnic groups, as in many African societies, the stages of growing up are clearly recognized, and the commonality of interests of each group is both acknowledged and institutionalized. There are four age grades, each grouping people into fifteen-year categories, from approximately 15 to 30 years, 30 to 45 years, 45 to 60 years, and over 60 years. The members of each age grade are expected to remain lifelong friends and to help one another in time of need. Members of each age grade have specific obligations to each other and designated roles within the village structure.

Members of the eldest group function as advisors; the middle groups of middle-aged and young married men actually administer village affairs. The youngest group, who in former times defended the village against attacks, takes care of collective village work projects, such as clearing land. Women, too, are divided into age groups, but they play less prominent roles than do men in the formal village structure. The establishment or passage of an age grade is the occasion for a grand celebration. Suppressed in many areas by colonial officials and missionaries, these rite-of-passage ceremonies are being revived as important features of village social life.

The eldest member within each age grade is its leader and spokesperson, an important functionary in village life. The leader of the eldest male age grade is the village patriarch. In the past, he was also the religious, judicial, and political leader, and he officiated in important religious rites. He made offerings to the spirits who protected the village and in times of misfortune asked their assistance.

Beginning in early colonial times, a younger man from the middle-aged group was designated to act as chief in place of the village patriarch in interactions with the colonial administration. This man became the village's functional political and juridical leader. This leader and the council of elders are now really the village decision makers, although they submit their decisions to the patriarch for his approval and accept his ultimate authority. The chief is chosen for his leadership qualities. He must be a good speaker and an equitable judge, with a thorough knowledge of the customs and beliefs of his people. In the past, the chief also had spokesmen or messengers who carried gold-headed canes as symbols of their office (Niangoran-Bouah 1969: 82–84; Yegnan 1968: 7–10).

THE CREATOR GOD
AND THE SPIRITS OF NATURE

Prior to the coming of the Prophet Harris, the Ebrié believed in an omniscient, omnipotent creator god, Yankan, who, like many African creator gods, was believed to have withdrawn from his initial intimate involvement in the everyday affairs of mortals. The explanation for this aloof relationship is that in the distant past, Yankan had been very much involved in the lives of his creatures—even to the extent of stipulating the quantity of futu, the staple dish, that a woman could prepare each day. It is said that one woman, secretly and rapidly, tried to pound more than her daily futu allotment. In her haste, she inadvertently struck Yankan, who was looking on, with her pounding stick. Infuriated by her act of disobedience, Yankan severed his close involvement with human life. Like other people around the world, the Ebrié interpreted their creator's apparent lack of concern with their problems as a manifestation of an imperfect relationship with him that was directly attributable to their own greed and willful behavior. Nevertheless, they continued to acknowledge his greatness and power, as well as his ability to bestow on them either hardship or prosperity (Amos-Djoro 1956: 39–40).

There were also lesser supernatural powers—nature spirits who were integrally involved in daily human life.[3] Their function was to insure health and prosperity and to protect people from evil. Villages had protective spirits to whom they appealed before major undertakings and in case of misfortune. There were also spirits associated with the natural elements of water, land, and plants that were involved with major subsistence activities.

Reigning in the lagoons where the Ebrié fish, for example, there were fishing spirits to whom people appealed for abundant catches. The neighboring Alladian, who also fish in the ocean, had a cult of a sea spirit. In addition to providing good catches and protecting the fishermen, she also assured their solidarity in this very dangerous work by punishing lazy people and those who failed to come to the aid of others. These beneficent spirits resided in highly valued elements of the natural environment. Before going off to war, young Adjoukrou men used to make sacrifices to the spirits who resided in the big trees that surround their villages and shielded them from attack. In addition to residing in the natural elements, beneficial spirits could also come to dwell in altars or masks that people made to house them.

These spirits required special recognition and observances. They demanded gifts of food and drink and sometimes sacrifices of animals as signs of proper human attention, respect, and gratitude for their assistance and protection. Certain foods, places, and activities associated with the spirits were designated as taboo. Whereas respect and compliance were expected to ensure prosperity, failure to obey the spirits' wishes brought dire consequences. In cases of misfortune or illness, lack of observance of a spirit's prescriptions and proscriptions was considered to be a probable cause. For the coastal people, such occurrences as drownings in the ocean or empty fishnets in the lagoons were the results of their own neglect of the spirits, whom they promptly acted to appease.

Certain spirits were worshiped on specially designated days of the week. Others were honored in less frequent ceremonies. The most important yearly village festival was the Yam Feast, at which the patriarch offered the first-harvested yams to the protective spirits to thank them for providing the harvest, and to seek their continuing assistance.

Periodically, or on the occasion of severe misfortune, villages held purification and blessing ceremonies. During them, people cleaned the village, throwing away all old and broken things, symbolically eliminating negative forces, and thus enabling the villagers to live together in peace and harmony. They then took purifying baths, dressed in symbolic white, and sprinkled the village with blessed water.

The cults of some spirits came to extend beyond specific village, and even ethnic areas, becoming regional as their effectiveness became known. Tano, for example, was a river spirit who acquired great fame in the coastal areas of both the Ivory Coast and the Gold Coast at the turn of the century. Members of Tano's priesthood wore white clothing and blessed the people who worshiped the spirit by sprinkling them with sacred water (Bureau 1971: 18). In about 1903 the cult of another spirit, Mando, spread not only to all of the Ebrié villages, but also to the other lagoons ethnic groups and then to the neighboring forest peoples. Especially effective in protecting people from witchcraft, Mando replaced many less effective spirits as the village guardian (Haliburton 1971: 62).

Another very important regional spirit, whom Georges Niangoran-Bouah characterized as the most important pre-Christian spirit, was Beugré. A powerful earth spirit with a vast sphere of competence, Beugré was invoked in cases of sterility; fishermen prayed to him for a plentiful catch; farmers prayed to him for a good harvest; and people in general prayed to him for good health, protection from enemies, victory in wars, and the end of epidemics. The altar to this great spirit was located about three hundred kilometers west of the lagoons area in the village of Bayibo, in the mountains of the Tabou region in the Kru area. Every year delegates from the lagoons ethnic groups went to the cave housing Beugré to ask the advice of, make requests of, sacrifice to, or thank the spirit. Leaving the supplicants outside the cave, the priest entered alone to consult the spirit on their behalf. He later emerged possessing both responses to their questions and objects invested with some of Beugré's power for his worshipers to take home with them (Niangoran-Bouah 1967: 125–27).

The Avikam, Dida, and other ethnic groups in the Grand Lahou area of the western end of the lagoons at one time worshiped another Kru spirit, Zri-Gnaba, who was located at Manjue in Cape Palmas, Liberia. This spirit also lived underground, and only his priest could descend to communicate with him. People traveled great distances to worship him, and also returned with objects filled with some of his protective power. One day each week was dedicated to Zri-Gnaba; on this day his worshipers did no work and wore only traditional handwoven cloth, rather than European-made materials (Haliburton 1971: 56).

The members of the clergy of each of these indigenous spirits had to learn the body of knowledge and the rituals associated with the spirit, and also had to undergo tests of their spiritual strength to determine their fitness for the priesthood (Amos-Djoro 1956: 54–55). Singers, female handclappers, instrument players, and sacrificers, who performed their designated tasks on special ritual occasions, were associated with the sanctuaries of some great spirits (Niangoran-Bouah 1967: 20).

A major way in which regional spirits became known in new areas was through the peregrinations of priests, who traveled from village to village, staying in each for a few weeks to teach the people how to worship the new spirit. Members of the clergy were extremely important and powerful because they mediated between the villagers and the spirits. The villagers' prosperity and happiness depended upon the priests' accurate interpretation of the desires of the spirits and on their own ability to fulfill these requirements.

WITCHCRAFT AND SPIRITUAL FORCE

The evil from which the spirits protected people was explained in terms of witchcraft, which was related to the concept of spiritual force. Each person had a spiritual force that was the body's animating and protective element. Health and prosperity were seen as visible manifestations of a person's strong spiritual force, which protected him or her from harm or evil. An elderly person was assumed to possess a strong spiritual force that had permitted longevity and the weathering of life's vicissitudes. Healers and religious leaders were also believed to have strong spiritual force that enabled them to lead, help, and protect others.

There were, however, people who used their spiritual force negatively, to the detriment of others. It was believed, for example, that the soul, wherein the spiritual force resided, could detach itself from the body. Dreams were explained as adventures of the soul when it left the body. One person's soul could harm the soul of another person by means of the evil of witchcraft, otherwise known as "cannibalism at a distance." The soul of the evil person was said to "eat" the soul of the victim, causing illness or killing the person. Witchcraft could make a woman unable to bear children, keep a student from succeeding in school, keep fish out of a neighbor's nets, or spoil another person's crops.

Thus, the concepts of witchcraft and of spiritual force provided the explanation for what might otherwise seem like the arbitrary character of good and bad fortune. They were ambivalent concepts, however. Prosperity might be evidence of the positive action of someone's strong spiritual force. But at the same time, prosperity could make people objects of suspicion and resentment and cause them to be targets of the witchcraft of jealous persons. The religious life of the lagoons people was therefore dynamic and pragmatic, as people sought the most effective spiritual protection, measurable in concrete results. Spirits that did not ensure prosperity and protection were superseded by those who proved themselves more effective.

From Sovereignty to Subjugation

The principal factor in setting the stage for the Prophet Harris's great appeal to the populations of the southern Ivory Coast was the turbulent political climate. At the time of Harris's arrival, the French had been established for two decades and were in the last stages of their military campaign to "pacify" the country.

By the middle of the nineteenth century, the Portuguese and the English had extensive commercial relations with the lagoons ethnic groups. They exchanged cloth, guns and gunpowder, and alcohol for ivory, gold, palm oil, and, until 1850, slaves. This was a period of prosperity for the coastal ethnic groups who served as middlemen between the European merchants and the ethnic groups of the interior (Amos-Djoro 1956: 28). The British controlled the trade along the coast, with Grand Lahou and Grand Bassam as major centers. The commercial language of the area was West African pidgin. The employees of the European businesses were, for the most part, British subjects from the Gold Coast and Sierra Leone.

"PEACEFUL" CONQUEST

In 1842, France established commercial treaties with chiefs in the important Ivory Coast centers of Fresco, Grand Lahou, Dabou, Grand Bassam, and Assinie. These commercial pacts stipulated that, to ensure the continuation of French trade, the Africans would trade only with the French and would welcome their missionaries. The French agreed, however, not to interfere with African village affairs.

To improve their commercial position, the French eventually decided to dispense with the coastal middlemen and to establish direct contact with the inland ethnic groups. This decision incurred the hostility of the lagoons groups, whose source of income was thereby threatened and who, in protest, began to pillage French convoys, steal from their warehouses, and fly the British flag.[4] The French retaliated against the lagoons people by brutally attacking them, often burning or bombarding villages and killing people in response to simple theft. Finally, treaties were signed between the French and a number of coastal villages, according to which the chiefs agreed to welcome French traders and to relinquish sovereignty over territory by selling to the French land for their forts. The phase of activity ending with the signing of the treaties was called by the French the period of "peaceful conquest" (Amon d'Aby 1951: 25; Amos-Djoro 1956: 29; Schnapper 1961: 146, 153, 157). Clearly, the conquest was more peaceful in theory than in practice.

The 1860s marked the beginning of a new phase in coastal trade relations. Palm oil prices in England declined, so the lagoons groups could obtain fewer European goods in exchange for their most important export item. Coastal chiefs allowed the French to establish trading houses on the coast, the better to assure their own supply of foreign merchandise; and under such favorable circumstances the French, spurred on by their apparent success at controlling the Africans, sought to extend the territory under their control (Schnapper 1961: 203, 208–9, 220).

The money and presents received from the French constituted a substantial portion of the income of some chiefs. With this new wealth some of them had multistoried houses built. In one village the chief built a European-style, two-story house with a large living room, three bedrooms, a balcony, an inside staircase, and walls decorated with mirrors. Other chiefs immediately sent their sons to Europe to be educated, but then feared that they were being held hostage because they stayed so long and refused to send any more children until the first ones returned home (Schnapper 1961: 63–64, 220).

Nothing in the chiefs' experience prepared them to understand the implications of ceding their land to the French. They expected to benefit and prosper, but they were instead impoverished; and subsequently they lost their political sovereignty as well as their economic independence. The rents they received for the land on which the French established commercial and military sites did not compensate for the wealth they lost by losing access to trade with the British and control over trade with the inland groups. A colonial official commented about this situaiton, "We have deceived these people, or they have deceived themselves about the results they should have gotten from our establishing ourselves among them" (Schnapper 1961: 63–65, 261–62).

Between 1890 and 1894, treaties with village chiefs established the geographical limits of French influence from the Republic of Liberia on the west to the British Gold Coast on the east. On 10 March 1893, the French declared the Ivory Coast a colony. Binger was appointed the first governor; Grand Bassam, the first capital. Following the 1899 epidemic in Grand Bassam, which killed 75 percent of the European population in just a few weeks, the capital was moved, in 1900, inland from the coast to Bingerville on the north bank of the Ebrié Lagoon (Amon d'Aby 1951: 25–26; Holas 1965: 45–46; Joseph 1917: 189).

"PEACEFUL" PENETRATION

The French characterized the period beginning in 1893 as that of "peaceful" penetration. Members of the colonial administration traveled through the colony with small groups of military escorts, seeking to present themselves not as oppressors, but as "protectors." They said that they sought to assure free trade, the punishment of pillagers, and freedom from aggression by other African or European (namely, British) invaders. French military posts were placed in various areas and were said by the colonial administration to be sources of defense and security for the Africans (*Côte d'Ivoire* 1964: 16). This form of "protective" occupation was relatively minimal, and to the extent that their presence did not interfere too much with the lives of the Africans, the French were received peacefully.

According to a French colonial administrator, when the French established the capital at Bingerville, most Ebrié were not overtly hostile, although the official judged that they were not pleased. He stated, with characteristic colonial ethnocentrism, "It obliged them, after all, to give up their savage practices" (Joseph 1917: 170). In response to the Ivorians' peaceful welcome, the French exploited, oppressed, and systematically brutalized them, leading one to question whose practices might most accurately be termed "savage."

In response to French interference in village affairs, M'Zaka, chief of Adjamé-Bingerville, encouraged the Ebrié to revolt. The French captured him and, on 31 October 1901, sent him to prison in the Congo. In the absence of his leadership, calm was restored in the village. In 1903, a few kilometers from Bingerville, the Ebrié of the village of Akoudio refused to clear the pathway for the construction of the telegraph lines and threatened the life of a colonial official in Bingerville. In retaliation, seventy colonial militiamen attacked the village, killing two men (Joseph 1917: 170–71).

Ebrié land continued to be summarily appropriated on subsequent occasions for the exigencies of the colonial administration. In 1907, the village of Akwadjamé was ordered to move to the east, and the village of Santé-Bingerville to move to the west, to allow more land for the expansion of the capital (Joseph 1917: 171; Niangoran-Bouah 1969: 57). The current capital, later established in a different location, was named Abidjan because it was built on the land of the Ebrié group known as the M'Bidjan.

During this period, feeling secure in their conquests, the French undertook to exploit systematically the economic possibilities of the colony. They initiated the cultivation of coffee and cocoa, forcing the Ivorians to work on the new plantations and on the development of more modern transportation and communications systems adapted to the economic and political needs of the colonial enterprise. Grand Bassam and Bingerville grew as population centers, and trade with Europe tripled in volume within a ten-year period. Progress—at least for the French colonialists—was apparent. To support national development projects, the French imposed a head tax in 1900, forcing the Ivorians into an unwanted and oppressive money economy. This forced labor for the benefit of the colonial enterprise, of course, worked to the detriment of the Ivorians' subsistence economy, further advancing the demise of their economic autonomy. Many chiefs, recognizing the tax as a blatant violation of their treaty agreements, sought to avoid payment, sometimes resorting to revolts that were brutally crushed by French military might.

"PACIFICATION"

The period of "peaceful" penetration lasted until 1908, when, with the appointment of Governor Gabriel Angoulvant, French colonial policy turned to an emphasis on "pacification." Although some parts of the country were entirely in French hands when Angoulvant took office, others were overtly hostile or virtually unknown, and thus not readily exploitable by the colonizers. In these sectors there was no trade, no tax money was collected, and there was little security for the French. The new thrust of colonial policy during this phase became that of establishing complete French control over the entire territory.

As the French stated their objectives, they sought to lead the Ivorians to make economic, as well as moral and social, progress. In theory, these goals were to be accomplished without significant damage to the indigenous life-style. There was almost no relationship between theory and practice, however. Basing their actions on French economic interests and a contempt for the African cultures, the colonialists deliberately sought to destroy the fundamental institutions of the indigenous societies to serve their own ends. J. F. Amon d'Aby states that "France solemnly declared her desire to observe and to apply the local customs whenever they were not contrary to the principles of what is generally considered civilized" (1951: 34). But "civilized," of course, meant to the colonialists that which was French.

The French endeavored to alter radically and rapidly the Ivorians' social structures and cultural values by introducing French education, reorganizing the system of justice, introducing new crops for commercial purposes, creating consumer demands, and setting up new lines of communication and transportation. Scattered small villages and campsites were regrouped into large villages located along the new roads, disrupting indigenous cultural and economic life; people were prohibited from moving around freely; chiefs were appointed who were responsive to the administration rather than responsible to their people; and leaders who objected to this oppression were exiled (Amon d'Aby 1951: 32–33). The colonizers also created new types of human relationships, both internal to the local societies—based on changed economic realities—and external to them—predicated on the subordination of all Africans to all Europeans.

Whenever the French felt it necessary, they used military expeditions to assure the Africans' compliance with their policies. By 1 May 1915, the large-scale military encounters required to force recalcitrant groups into submission had ended and the colony was declared "pacified." There still remained for the French colonial administration the tasks of consolidating their accomplishments by winning the allegiance of the Ivorians and of stimulating them to work for the economic progress of the colony and the metropole.

Many colonial subjects, of course, did not willingly accept pacification. The disarming of the Ivorians was still going on in 1917, and some chiefs and important elders near Abidjan were punished in 1918 for not paying taxes. The Ebrié village of Locodjoro remained refractory, and many people fled the village in order to avoid paying taxes (Ivory Coast, Rapport d'Ensemble, 1917, and Rapport Politique, 1918).

As a result of the administration's demands, agricultural production increased, and the colony began making more rapid economic progress. By 1917, both Grand Bassam and Bingerville had cobblestone roads, electricity, and some cars; and the first airplane landed in Grand Bassam in 1926 (Holas 1965: 47; Joseph 1917: 203).

THE CATHOLIC FAILURE

In 1895, Governor Binger had summoned Catholic missionaries from the Missions Africaines de Lyon to come to provide churches and schools to make the Ivorians into loyal and obedient French subjects. The arrival of these missionaries marked the third attempt on the part of Catholic missionaries to implant Christianity in the Ivory Coast territory. The first attempt had been made by Capuchin missionaries in July 1637 in Assinie. Received in splendid style by the local king, they told him that they wanted to settle there to teach the Africans new knowledge and new mysteries. The king designated land upon which they could establish a mission. The following Sunday they planted a cross and celebrated a mass that the king and many people attended. The missionaries began teaching about the Bible, but the Africans apparently lost interest. Some members of the missionary contingent died from unfamiliar maladies; others departed (Mouézy 1954: 93). A second attempt lasting from 1841 to 1844 was equally unsuccessful (Yando 1970: 11).

Thus, when the missionaries summoned by Binger arrived, the only African Christians they found were the Methodist Africans from the Gold Coast and Sierra Leone who worked for British firms. They formed a distinct community, however, and did not try to evangelize the Ivorians. French missionary activities were limited to the coastal areas because of the lack of roads and transportation, as well as because of the missionaries' apprehensions about the peoples of the interior. When the missionaries did succeed in convincing coastal villagers to abandon their religions in order to learn about the missionaries' faith, the Africans often found the process of transition too slow. Fearing the ineffectiveness of the new faith, they returned to their old, familiar ways.

The epidemic in Grand Bassam killed a number of the missionaries and provided a major setback for the mission efforts (Amos-Djoro 1956: 110, 116; Bianquis 1924: 1086–1106; Haliburton 1971: 40–41). Given the Ivorian pragmatism about spiritual protection, the death of the very people who had come to teach them a new religion was seen as a clear sign of its inadequacy.

Thus despite their efforts to spread Christianity while the colonial administration established its military control of the colony, the Catholic missionaries had very limited success. By the time the colony was declared pacified, even after two decades of ardent evangelizing involving a total of twenty-three missionaries, there were only four hundred baptized Christians and eleven hundred additional people being instructed for baptism (Bianquis 1924: 1088).

CHAPTER 3

The Religious Revolution

A Tidal Wave of Conversion

A 1915 political report furnishes a colonial administrator's brief résumé of the phenomenal impact in the Ivory Coast of the Prophet William Wade Harris:

> The arrival in the Colony, in 1914,[1] of an African named Harris, native of Liberia, and calling himself "prophet," had led, in the coastal region, to a movement of conversion among the animist populations who, under the influence of the messenger of God, burned their fetishes.[2] The hypnotic action of the "prophet" was very effective in the administrative regions of Assinie, Bassam, the Lagoons, Lahou, and in parts of the Indénié and N'Zi-Comoë administrative regions, involving the conversion of about 100,000 people. Churches, simple huts made of leaves and branches, were constructed in all of the villages. Harris baptized, and promised his proselytes a marvelous afterlife provided that they worked diligently, were temperate, did not steal, did only good, and submitted to the orders of the authorities. His actions were observed closely by the government, the administrators and the chiefs of posts, particularly because it was essential, at the time when the European war had just broken out, to maintain a state of perfect tranquility among our subjects, and especially to inhibit the circulation of false or alarming rumors.
>
> The movement provoked by Harris unfortunately involved a number of imitators, or "sons of God," [who were] unemployed clerks seeking to find resources in the exploitation of the credulity of the natives. Many were brought before the courts of the subdivisions, where they were charged with swindling, and to

avoid all agitation, Harris himself was requested to carry the good word to his native country. He left the colony and was not heard of again until the end of the year when he appeared at the border of the administrative region of Bas-Cavally,[3] where he was invited not to cross the border again. The action of the "prophet" had no other consequences than to lead the natives living near the centers to attend, in a bit larger numbers, the Protestant and Catholic churches. [Ivory Coast, Situation Politique, 1915]

According to political reports of the period, Harris entered the Ivory Coast late in 1913. Walking along the coast with his two female companions, he stopped in villages and towns to preach the message that people must learn to worship the Christian god. Harris's presence was first documented with the statement of an English commercial agent, who said that in three days Harris had turned the town of Fresco, formerly "sunk in debased superstition and fetish worship," into a nominally Christian town (Platt 1934: 34). As a result of such success, Harris's fame spread to other villages, where he was described variously as "a messenger of God" and "a great fetish[er]" (Haliburton 1971: 49).

The prophet continued to the Avikam town of Ebonou, where there had been no Christian missionary influence. The spirits worshiped there included both Mando and Zri-Gnaba. Harris convinced the townspeople to cease worshiping those spirits, to destroy their altars, and to let him baptize them in the name of his god (Haliburton 1971: 49–51).

In Ebonou, Harris encountered some of the Methodist clerks from the Gold Coast and Sierra Leone. He convinced them to aid him in his campaign of conversion and left them to carry on his work there. He empowered one clerk, A. E. M. Brown, to baptize the people he had not reached, and named another clerk, J. W. (Sam) Refell, to assist Brown. Along with other English-speaking Methodists recruited to aid them, they continued Harris's work of baptizing converts and destroying traditional cult objects. They taught Methodist hymns translated into Avikam, the Ten Commandments, the Lord's Prayer, and elements of Christian practice. The villagers built churches in which services led by Harris's new disciples sometimes lasted from six in the morning until six in the evening, without stopping for meals (Haliburton 1971: 50–51; Joseph 1917: 157).

Harris's success in Ebonou was such that he was summoned further inland to the Dida town of Lozoua. The people of Lozoua had first learned of the prophet in a letter from his disciple Brown to a friend in the town, telling of Harris's remarkable success in Ebonou. There Harris had overcome the power of the traditional spirits and their priests and had rid the town of the abuses of the traditional religious system. Lozoua was, at the time, embroiled in a complicated series of witchcraft accusations, because the chief's daughter had allegedly been killed through witchcraft.

Harris convinced the villagers to accept his baptism, telling them that it would protect them from harm, and he burned the masks and altars in which the spirits that had not succeeded in providing this protection resided. The religious objects located in the chief's compound were the first to be burned. These objects were associated with the powerful spirit, Mando, as well as with Gboualegbé and Brengba, which had been brought from Cape Palmas. After the chief's ritual artifacts had been destroyed, the villagers' religious objects were added to the flames (Haliburton 1971: 52–54).

Although the residents of Lozoua had defied the traditional spirits, surrounding villagers preferred to maintain their beliefs and practices. Their religious leaders tried to make Harris sick, but, when they were unsuccessful, conceded that the spiritual being he represented was more powerful than theirs. Harris told the villagers to build a church and to worship his god by singing their own religious songs with the addition of God's name. When people asked him who would teach them after his departure, he replied that he had commissioned Christian British subjects to continue his work and to keep them on the right path until men with Bibles came to teach them (Haliburton 1971: 54–55).

After about one month in Lozoua, Harris was arrested by colonial officers and taken to Grand Lahou to prison. After he explained his religious mission to a colonial administrator, he was labeled a "harmless maniac" and released into the custody of some influential Africans who had interceded for him. One explanation for the arrest was that a group of traditional religious leaders, afraid that Harris would make them lose their power and influence, had turned the French against him. Unable to combat Harris's power, the village priests told the colonial commander that the prophet was deceiving people in order to take their money, and should be driven away (Haliburton 1971: 55–56).

In effect, by imprisoning Harris and releasing him so quickly, the French unwittingly added to his renown and reputation. The belief developed, and is still held by Harrists, that the prophet was released from prison miraculously. According to John Ahui, patriarch of the Harrist church, Harris was initially locked into his cell by an African guard. Shortly thereafter, the cell door opened by itself and Harris walked out. The French commander, suspecting collusion between the two Africans, locked Harris into the cell himself, keeping a close watch on anyone who might open the door. Again, the cell door opened by itself and Harris walked out. Even the French commander was then forced to conclude, according to Ahui, that Harris was not an ordinary man, and "not a man who could be held in prison, but surely a messenger of God."

At the time of the political report of July 1914, local authorities in the Cercle de Grand Lahou were still not sure of the nature of Harris's intentions. Then in the last stages of "pacifying" the Ivorians, the French monitored very closely the mass activities he inspired. Because of what they saw as his positive effects on the "moral evolution" of the Ivorians, colonial officials in Lahou were divided over whether to send him away or leave him alone. They watched to see if his activities were taking a political turn, but concluded that he and his disciples were merely baptizing people. This political report highlighted Harris's success in Ebonou and Lozoua and his potential usefulness for the purposes of the colonial administration: "The battle that we have waged against the fetishers, particularly because of their use of ordeals and because of the silent battle that they have led against our authority, had not led to any conclusive results at all, in spite of our courts and the severe punishment inflicted; in a few days this native obtained this unhoped-for result" (Ivory Coast, Rapport Politique, Cercle de Grand Lahou, 11 July 1914).

When Harris left the Cercle de Grand Lahou to continue his journey eastward, his influence there persisted. After his departure, his Methodist clerk-disciples, following his example, continued to teach his converts as he had directed them, baptizing the people who came seeking the prophet. Harris proceeded to Kraffy in the Cercle des Lagunes, at the border of the Cercle de Lahou, in December 1913. As rumors of his power spread, delegations came from all over the lagoons area seeking his baptism (Haliburton 1971: 60–67).

A Gold Coast trader named Goodman, a practicing Methodist in the Ebrié village of Audoin, near Abidjan, sent two messengers to see the prophet during his brief visit in the town of Jacqueville, to request that he visit Audoin. Harris did not go, but sent a Bible and requested that Goodman himself begin baptizing people. Goodman succeeded in gaining credibility with the villagers as one commissioned by the prophet, who thus shared some of his spiritual authority. The inhabitants of Audoin, at the insistence of the French Catholic missionaries, had previously burned the objects in which their protective spirits resided. However, receiving no satisfying spiritual replacement from the foreign missionaries, and finding themselves in hardship, they had resumed their former practices. Under Goodman's leadership the villagers again burned their masks and altars, and two traditional priests became ministers in the new religion (Haliburton 1971: 68–70).

The Power of Baptism

The Prophet Harris was described as a man of striking appearance with white hair and a white beard, in sharp contrast to his strong, attractive, ebony face. He was said to have a very imposing personality and a thundering voice. Dressed in a long white gown, with a black scarf around his neck and a small white hat on his head, he carried a stafflike bamboo cross, an English Bible, a gourd rattle wrapped in a net of beads, and a small gourd bowl used as a receptacle for baptismal water.

Harris and his similarly attired female companions stopped at the entrance to each village or town and, to the accompaniment of their rattles, sang religious hymns until they attracted attention. Sometimes their arrival would already have been announced by a messenger, in which case the villagers would be prepared and would gather to greet them. Harris preached about the abuses of the traditional religion and the benefits of Christianity, convincing people to destroy the material objects in which their protective spirits resided. He baptized those who were willing as a symbol of their newly established relationship with his god.

Church patriarch John Ahui described the situation into which Harris came, and his method:

> Before the arrival of Harris, everything was based on fetishes, amulets, everything that was against the life of man. There was no one who could tell people that God existed.
>
> When the first whites arrived, they came with their own church, their own faith, and their own education. They said, "stop worshiping fetishes and we will teach you something different." At the bidding of the whites our ancestors buried or burned their fetishes, or threw them into the sea, but then they had nothing with which to replace them. Then they took their fetishes back.
>
> They thought that because they had no more fetishes, they had no strength and nothing worked well. They brought back their fetishes and with them they found their strength and freedom again.
>
> Each time the whites told them to get rid of their fetishes, they tried to, but they received no replacement.
>
> Then Harris came. It was the same thing—the same words. "Abolish your fetishes. They will not help you. I will give you something with which to replace them that will protect you— baptism. Do not practice fetishism, it will not help you. Worship God. He will do good for you."
>
> Harris said that once you are baptized, the fetishes will have no more power over you. Baptism will change your life. You should build a temple and worship God. [Personal interview, 19 January 1972]

A major element of Harris's technique of conversion, of key importance in his success, was his provision of an immediate replacement for the system of belief and protection that he asked the Ivorians to relinquish. For Harris and his converts, baptism was primordial. During a meeting in Bingerville, the Catholic missionary Father Hartz asserted to the prophet that he should not baptize. Harris's response was to lead hundreds of people to the priest for him to baptize. Hartz objected that they could not be baptized until they had been taught about and understood something of Christianity, and had understood and accepted the meaning of baptism. Harris insisted that God would take care of the teaching, and that he had been sent to baptize everyone in the Ivory Coast who had not already been baptized by the Catholic fathers: "Christ orders me to do so. I must give these crowds a preservative against the influence of the fetish that they are leaving. This preservative is the Water and the power it acquires at the touch of my cross" (van Bulck 1961: 122–23).

Harris understood that he could not hope to convince people to abandon their traditional beliefs and practices without immediately providing something stronger to take their place, replete with a system of explanations and sanctions that would prohibit the converts from returning to their previous system. Unlike the missionaries, who insisted that instruction must precede baptism, the Prophet Harris baptized people as soon as they agreed to the basic tenets that he preached: to cease worshiping their indigenous spirits and to destroy all of the objects in which they resided, to respect the Sabbath, and to lead "a Christian life." A provision of this baptism was that, should they have recourse to their traditional religion, or in other ways sin against God, he would punish them. Thus, Harris's baptism represented both a purification from past sins and a protection against evil, and also a nonrescindable commitment to living a "Christian" life.

Many stories continue to be told about the manifestations of Harris's power and about what happened to people who disobeyed him. Some people say that everything he said came true within twenty-four hours. Others say that as he approached a village, the protective spirits fled, leaving empty of power the material objects in which they had resided. According to one Harrist minister: "The fetishes said to their masters, 'I do not have any more power because there is a Great Spirit coming who is more powerful than I am. I am going away to the North.'"

It is said in the Lahou area that some of the people who brought Harris their religious objects to destroy kept a few hidden in the forest as insurance, just in case Harris's god failed to protect them fully. As Harris was burning the objects brought before him, those hidden in the forest also mysteriously burst into flames. Harrists say that when the prophet entered some villages, altars and houses containing masks caught fire from his mere proximity. Another story is told of a man who came to receive Harris's baptism, but left a prized mask at home, not daring to part with it. As he stepped into his canoe to return home, he fell dead.

One village that did not respond positively to Harris's teachings was said to have been subsequently attacked by baboons. In a village in which half the people wanted to be baptized and the other half did not, Harris is said to have called down water from the sky on only the wise half, in order to baptize them. In another village, some people accepted Harris's baptism and remained faithful, whereas others returned to their previous religious practices. Harrists say that fishermen from the latter group began to pull in empty nets, and farmers' crops withered, whereas the prophet's converts experienced prosperity.

An event that took place in the village of Bonoua won the Prophet Harris a great deal of esteem in the Bassam, Assinie, and Lagoons administrative districts. This important village had a strong spirit that had been introduced by an Abidji man named Labri. The villagers gave Labri a great deal of wealth to keep Harris from entering Bonoua. Harris did enter and found Labri dancing around the building in which the spirit was housed. Upon seeing Harris, Labri fled into the forest and was never heard from again. Harris told the villagers to burn all of their altars and masks, and then he baptized everyone, including Labri's wife and nephew. As word of his conquest spread, people came from far away to seek him out (Joseph 1917: 158–59).

Other events added to his fame. Harris stated that a crew that was unloading and reloading a ship in the harbor was offending God by working on Sunday. A few days later the boat burned mysteriously. Administrator Cécaldi of Grand Bassam called Harris a troublemaker and made him leave the town. The European died a week after his inhospitable treatment of God's messenger (van Bulck 1961: 12). The prophet's converts viewed such just and prompt retribution as a clear indication of the power of Harris's god.

A very important attribute of Harris's power was that it was also effective with respect to the Europeans, a domain in which the indigenous religious system had proven itself inadequate. Traditional religious leaders had been unsuccessful in protecting the Ivorians from defeat by the French. Those traditional priests who had led revolts against the French had been imprisoned or exiled along with the chiefs who refused to capitulate. Combined, they numbered more than two hundred. Now an African had come along with a spiritual power far superior to that of the traditional system, and he had proven its effectiveness in coping with Europeans and the accoutrements of their world.

The Power of Pragmatism

In addition to his spiritual message, the Prophet Harris also shared with the Ivorians a more pragmatic message, one based on both his Protestant orientation and his own background. He told the Ivorians to work diligently every day but Sunday. He told them to send their children to school so that they could learn to read the Word of God, contained in the Bible.

The colonialists had been trying to encourage or, if necessary, coerce the Ivorians to work on their development projects. They also urged the Africans to send their children to the missionary schools so that they could acquire the skills of literacy and the knowledge of French that would make them useful to the colonial endeavor, and so that they could learn an appreciation for French culture.

The Ivorians had been recalcitrant on both counts. They preferred working on their own activities, for their own benefit, to working under conditions of coercion at tasks that had no apparent meaning or benefit to themselves. They preferred to educate their children into their own life-style as they had always done, rather than sending them to some foreigners whose motives obviously did not serve the Africans' interests. Just as they had done in the spiritual sphere, however, they began to obey the prophet.

Harrists say that the prophet also told the Ivorians that if they lived as he told them, working diligently and worshiping his god properly for seven years, at the end of this period they would be able to have everything the Europeans had. They could attain the same knowledge and material wealth, live in two-story houses, and eat at the same table with Europeans. Thus, certain elements of the European life-style provided models to which the Ivorians could aspire.

One may imagine the attraction of such a message to the Ivorians, who were undoubtedly impressed by the novelties of French technology, to say nothing of their military might, and who realized that the colonizers' superior living conditions were the result of the Africans' own labor. Hence, the powerful prophet who had provided convincing proof of his spiritual system also offered them a pragmatic program for material improvement.

Harris preached the Golden Rule, "Love thy neighbor," to the diverse ethnic groups who came to hear him, some of whom had had hostile relations with each other. Harrists say that before the prophet came, a stranger or a member of a different ethnic group could not go into some villages and feel safe. They also maintain that, had Harris not succeeded in influencing people of different ethnic groups to live together peacefully, Abidjan could never have been constructed, and the Ivory Coast could not have attained its present level of development. By teaching people that they must all worship the same god and regard people of different ethnic groups as members of their human family, then, Harris created a situation in which people could live together in harmony.

Spreading the Faith

Conscious of the urgency and the enormity of his mission, and persecuted by the colonial authorities, Harris did not stay in any one place for very long. His longest stays were in major villages and towns where people came from distant areas to hear him. The prophet had two methods of ensuring that his converts would continue in the direction he had shown them, and of spreading his message to areas he was unable to visit. When he met Methodist clerks whom he considered to be responsible Christians, he requested them to baptize people and to organize churches in which to teach the new converts to sing, pray, and worship the Christian god.

In view of the brief time that Harris spent in the Ivory Coast, and the number of people he is credited with having baptized, it becomes evident that his clerk-disciples baptized many people in areas from which the prophet had already departed or which he never visited. These clerk-disciples assured the continuity of the movement he had begun. Because Harris's activities had destroyed the Ivorians' trust in the power of their indigenous religion, they were receptive to the disciples who were bringing them the Christianity he espoused. The clerks also helped to extend the movement inland from the coast to areas the prophet had not reached.

Harris's other method of assuring the perpetuation of his work was to choose leaders from the delegations from different villages who came to see him, whom he charged with the task of teaching his message to their fellow villagers. He told them to develop a religious leadership for the village consisting of a minister and twelve apostles to administer the church. He sometimes made bamboo crosses for them, as symbols of their mission to perpetuate his teachings.

Returning home, these representatives would tell other villagers that they must burn their traditional religious objects, and would teach them to worship the Christian god, as they themselves had learned in the brief period during which they had seen Harris or one of his disciples. If they were near one of the churches attended by the Methodist clerks, these new religious leaders would go to listen to the sermon and later share with other villagers what they had learned. Some groups of villagers even traveled long distances by canoe to attend one of these churches. In this way, Harris's religious revolution extended to areas that he never visited, and the indigenous religion gave way to new forms.

To the Gold Coast and Back

Harris continued eastward from the lagoons area across the border into the southwest corner of the Gold Coast colony, where he spent three months. Missionaries had been in this area of the Gold Coast for years, and there were African Protestant ministers. They had succeeded in Christianizing many Fanti, but neither foreign missionaries nor African ministers had been able to convince the Nzima people to abandon their religion. During his brief stay, however, Harris made many converts among the Nzima.[4]

As in the Ivory Coast, Harris preached his message, burned religious objects, and baptized. He insisted, however, that he was not a minister and did not intend to found a church. He directed the people he baptized to the existing churches. Although the missionaries heartily appreciated his assistance, and some Protestants considered him a true messenger of God sent to help them convert people, they also realized that "where the prophet's work ended, the pastor's toil began" (Armstrong 1920: 39–40, 47).

Now that they had their converts, they had to teach them to be Christians. In 1913, one Methodist mission had 633 active members. In 1915, after Harris's visit, the number climbed to 2,387, and by 1921 it had reached 4,737 (Haliburton 1971: 157). One missionary received a letter summoning him to come help minister to 2,000 people who were seeking admission to church. He found upon his arrival not 2,000 but 8,000 people, all eager to be taught (Armstrong 1920: 39–40, 47).

Because of the crowds drawn to the town of Axim, Harris's presence became a source of concern to the British colonial government. There was not enough food in the town for such numbers; they posed sanitation problems; and because of Harris's insistence upon respect for the Sabbath, they refused to load or unload ships on Sundays. Accordingly, a government representative invited him to leave. The Gold Coast government later admitted that Harris had had an amazing effect in introducing more sanitary conditions into the towns he visited, and attributed to him the fact that the people had abandoned their traditional religions and had built Christian churches and schools in their villages (Bureau 1971: 28; Haliburton 1971: 87–90).

During his short stay in the Gold Coast, Harris's popularity soared in the Ivory Coast as word of his power spread, and when he returned there he was very much in demand. He found delegations of Agni and Nzima from the eastern part of the country waiting to take him to their villages. When he arrived in Bingerville, he stayed for six weeks, baptizing many people who had come from as much as two hundred miles away by foot or canoe.

The French authorities were also awaiting the prophet's return. Because of the unprecedented human activity he had provoked in most of the coastal area, Harris was summoned to explain his activities to Governor Angoulvant in the autumn of 1914. The governor was favorably impressed with Harris and pleased because his exhortations were in the interests of the colonial effort. Harris had achieved better results, and more quickly and easily, than the colonialists had obtained through brutality and bloodshed. He had modified the power of the religious leaders who had led opposition to the French; persuaded hostile ethnic groups that it was against the Will of God, as expressed in the Golden Rule, for them to fight among themselves; and urged people to work hard and to accept the authority of the colonial officers.

Colonial officers indicated with pleasure that a major result of the prophet's activities was that his converts in some areas had become diligent workers, and expressed hope that the spreading of the religious movement to new areas would have the same salutory effect. Indeed, it was these aspects of his impact that convinced the administration to allow the prophet to continue his spiritual mission.

While he was in Bingerville, Harris had an audience with Father Joseph Gorju, leader of the Catholic mission in the colony, who was also favorably impressed by his contact with the prophet. There Harris attended Catholic masses and directed his converts to the Catholic churches. The missionaries were pleased that he was communicating a Christian message to those people they had been unsuccessful in reaching. Gorju wrote of Harris: "The triumphal journey continues, and innumerable crowds flock in great numbers toward the 'great man.' Our missions are also besieged. People ask for a medal, a protective token of some sort. On Sunday, our churches are unable to contain the congregation that invades the entire surroundings from the break of day" (1915: 267).

One may suspect that the Ivorians saw the direct link between the material objects containing spirits that they had just destroyed and the new ones, the Catholic medals they sought, which they assumed to be more powerful. Although these medals were reminiscent of their former "fetishes," the Ivorians assumed that they were somehow different and acceptable, because they were from the church to which the prophet had led his converts.

Thus, in August 1914, when the chief of the colonial administrative post in the town of Dabou toured the coastal area of his district, he found the altars and masks of the indigenous spirits destroyed, churches built, and people practicing "Protestantism." According to a political report from October 1914, "The only item even worth indicating is that Adzopé has been converted to the new religion." This, it was hoped, would have the effect of getting people to work regularly (Ivory Coast, Rapport Politique, Cercle des Lagunes,

October 1914). Another political report, from November 1914, said:

> In the course of this trimester the religious propaganda, or rather contagion, spread throughout the district. The conversion of the ferocious inhabitants of the forest to the religion of the Prophet Harris has had until now only beneficial consequences, of which the principal one is the destruction of the fetishes. It is probable that the success of the son of God will only last for a while, but it nonetheless constitutes an interesting event, the results of which must be carefully monitored. [Ivory Coast, Rapport Politique du 3e trimester 1914, 5 November 1914]

After leaving Bingerville, Harris traveled west toward the Cercle de Lahou, passing through territory he had already visited and preaching and baptizing with great success. The political report from Grand Lahou for December 1914 reported that the Harrist movement had grown tremendously during the month because of the return of the prophet, who had baptized the many people who had come from afar to hear him. He stayed in Grand Lahou only briefly, however. Having arrived the evening of 10 December, he was asked to leave on 12 December by the colonial administrator (Ivory Coast, Rapport Politique, Cercle de Grand Lahou, 31 December 1914).

The positive activity that took place during Harris's absence from the Ivory Coast was a result both of the impetus he had given and of the continued efforts of his disciples. The news had spread that traditional religious objects would burst into flames in his presence, that people who accepted his baptism insincerely would suffer the results immediately and visibly, that colonial officials could not keep him in prison, and that an administrator who had mistreated him had died for his deeds. Interest in the man and his message spread, and people sought to be baptized and to learn about Harris's god. People who had originally been unreceptive to his message and people who had heard from afar of a man bringing a new and stronger god tried to find him. In many instances they found not the prophet himself, but one of the disciples who had been empowered by Harris to extend and continue his work.

They went to Brown at Ebonou, and to a man known only as "Papa" at Grand Lahou. The two of them baptized thousands of people whose conversions were attributed to Harris. Many people were also baptized by Victor Nivri, the Catholic chef de canton from the Alladian town of Addah who, seeing Alladians, Adjoukrous, and Ebriés passing through on the way to Grand Lahou to be baptized, requested authorization from Brown and began to baptize also. Addah became a center of pilgrimage, and Nivri also traveled to other towns to baptize.

A group of young men from the Adjoukrou village of Mopoyeme was sent to Grand Lahou to ascertain the source of the religious excitement about which they had heard. There the men were baptized by Papa. They returned to Mopoyeme with the news, and the rest of the villagers went to Addah, which was closer, to be baptized by Nivri. Nivri's costume replicated Harris's, and his conversions are reported to have been as spectacular as the prophet's, with people guilty of evil going into convulsions before him and then being calmed with his holy water.

Many Adjoukrous, Abbeys, Attiés, and Ebriés were converted in Adjoukrou country by the disciples Papa and Sam, who are also reported to have healed people. Sam is said to have made a foray into Abbey country in defiance of an order from a colonial officer not to do so because he was teaching people to pray and sing in English, the language of their colonial rivals, rather than in French. In the opinion of the French, this was a subversive act (Haliburton 1971: 93–96, 105–7).

It may seem curious that Harris's disciples had such great success, inasmuch as they, unlike the prophet, were only secular agents who had not received any divine revelation or direct mandate from God. There are several probable reasons for their ability to duplicate the success of the prophet himself.

The people who had heard the news about the Prophet Harris from afar knew nothing about him except what he was doing. They did not know what he looked like or even, sometimes, his name. Thus, when they found someone who was doing what they expected the "great fetisher" or the "messenger of God" to be doing, that person was accepted as the object of their search.

Haliburton notes that some Abbeys who claim to have been baptized by Harris in Grand Lahou were apparently baptized by Brown or another of the prophet's disciples, because Harris was not in Grand Lahou at the time (Haliburton 1971: 125). In fact, during his two visits to Grand Lahou, Harris had spent only a total of about four days. He apparently did not preach the first time or even receive a positive reception. It is thus evident that the great majority of his conversions in the Lahou area were really the work of his disciples.

Harris's disciples did the same things he had done: they preached the same message, burned indigenous religious objects, and converted or overcame the power of traditional priests. Some disciples are reported to have healed, some wore garments similar to Harris's, and most of them were also Protestant. Most spoke English and carried an English Bible like Harris, and they accomplished the same results as he did, thus perpetuating his movement.

Expulsion and Persecution

On 16 December 1914, the French colonial administration acted to expel Harris. According to the account reported by Haliburton, the prophet was probably arrested at Kraffy, where he had gone after being ordered to leave Grand Lahou, and then taken back to Grand Lahou. From there he and his female companions were taken to Dabou and then to Abidjan, where they were jailed and beaten so severely that one of his companions died of the effects shortly after returning home. They were then placed on a boat for Liberia, sailing from Bassam before crowds who had come to witness their departure (1971: 139–41).

Another version of the prophet's departure, which Haliburton characterizes as a later attempt by the colonial administration to portray itself in a more favorable light, is widely reported in literature about Harris. According to this version, Harris was preaching on the beach at Port Bouet, near Abidjan, in about April 1915. A French official named Paoli waited until he had finished preaching, allowed his own African servants to be baptized by him, and then informed the prophet that he would have to leave the country. Harris acquiesced with dignity and was escorted politely to the border (Haliburton 1971: 141–42). The timing of this version is contradictory. The French vice-consul in Monrovia, asked by the French in December 1914 to furnish information about Harris's activities in Liberia, reported in February 1915 that Harris had been in Cape Palmas in January after his expulsion from the Ivory Coast (Haliburton 1971: 141–42).

The next step for the colonial administration was the attempt at full-scale destruction of Harris's movement, out of fear of the expression of African autonomy it represented. Colonial guards circulated in the lagoons area and destroyed or forbade the use of the churches that Harris's converts had built for the practice of their new religion. The French had begun to view the new churches as a threat to their control over their subjects. Although the churches professed to be Christian, they were entirely African religious institutions with no European, loyal to the colonial cause, at the helm.

With their numbers reduced from thirteen to six, and two of their eight mission stations closed because of the mobilization for World War I, the Catholic missionaries began to see the proliferation of Harris's Protestant clerk-disciples as part of a conspiracy, part of a deliberate attack on them in their weakened state, and as an attempt to implant in the colony their mortal foe—Protestantism. Although Harris had tried to maintain good rapport with the Catholic missionaries, attending their churches and sending them many converts, Father Gorju, who had previously spoken so positively of the prophet and who continued to be pleased to receive his converts, now wrote of him: "Soon the second act of the drama is going to begin. It is also the moment when the enemy's plan begins to make itself visible. The Prophet retreats a bit into the shadow; the extras replace him on the stage. . . . The Protestants had certainly not had the intention of working in our favor" (1915: 267).

Jean Bianquis, a Protestant missionary, commented cynically on the Catholic reaction: "The personal initiative of a Black man who believes that he has received a divine vocation is transformed into a kind of vast plot, promoted by a mysterious and maleficent international power (Protestantism)" (1924: 1103).

The Prophet of African Autonomy

From August to November of 1914, both colonial administrators and Catholic missionaries expressed favorable reactions concerning the constructive effects of the prophet's activities for the colonial effort. Why, then, was he expelled from the colony?

One important external factor influencing the decision was the mobilization of personnel for World War I. Men were recruited both from the ranks of the colonial officials and militia and from the numbers of the missionaries, weakening the colonial apparatus. Whereas the administrative officials strongly objected to the influence of a foreign African over their subjects, the Catholic missionaries were most concerned, it seems, with Harris's Protestantism, which represented what they considered to be an enemy force.

Also significant for the administration was the fact that Harris's message, as it was understood by some groups in the interior, rather than urging cooperation with the authorities, was anti-French. A political report from Lakota, in Dida country, from August 1914, said that many of the people in that area believed what they had always hoped for—that the Europeans would leave to fight a war in their own country. In the villages where this belief was strong, the people, once cooperative under duress, became rebellious again (Ivory Coast, Rapport Politique, Poste de Lakota, August 1914).

From Divo and Grand Lahou came rumors that the Germans had conquered the French and destroyed Paris, and that the French, because of their military defeat, were leaving the Ivory Coast. Colonial officers made visits to many villages to convince the people that even though some Europeans were closing their stores and leaving because of the war mobilization, the whites were still in control (Ivory Coast, Rapport Politique, District de Divo, September 1914, and Rapport Politique, Cercle de Grand Lahou. 31 August 1914). The Abbey believed that Harris would help them to chase the French away (Yando 1970: 94). East of the Cercle des Lagunes, in the Cercle du N'Zi-Comoë, to which the prophet's influence had only begun to spread on his return from the Gold Coast, some Agni believed that, having become Christians, they were free and no longer had to take orders from anyone. Accordingly, they ceased to pay taxes and do forced labor (Haliburton 1971: 126, 128).

Because of the new emphases Harris's message had acquired in some areas, and its debilitating effect on French control, and partly because much of the religious activity was led by Africans who were subjects of a competing colonial power, the French decided to expel the prophet from the Ivory Coast. Although never denying the positiveness of Harris's effect on the coastal populations, the colonial administrators obviously found that he had already accomplished his mission to a sufficient extent.

The French were finishing their "pacification" of the colony and the consolidation of their control over the entire territory. They had succeeded in dominating the many ethnic groups of the country through military force. Their efforts to convince the Ivorians of the superiority of French culture and to impose French values had failed, as evidenced by the missionaries' efforts.

Harris, a single, barefoot, elderly African religious leader, inspired by a divine vision, represented a very real threat to the French colonial system. Their suspicions of him led them to keep him under constant surveillance in an attempt to detect evidence of his increased politicization, to feature him constantly in their administrative reports, to hamper his movements, to persecute him, and eventually to expel him.

It is apparent that the colonial administration in the Ivory Coast knew very little about Harris's background. Had they been aware of his antigovernmental political activities in Liberia, they would undoubtedly have been even more wary of his motives than they were. Pierre Benoit, in discussing Harris's effect on people in the Ivory Coast, supports the French fear of the prophet's potential power by saying, "In 1914 one word from him would have thrown the Ivory Coast into rebellion" (F. Walker 1927b: 111).

In a very brief time, then, this single individual had convinced more than a hundred thousand people to abandon the religious system that had formed the basis of their world view and to adopt the beginnings of a new one, of which he had demonstrated the effectiveness. Harris's religion was effective not only because it proved stronger than the indigenous religions, but also because it provided solutions to the distressing circumstances of the oppressive colonial situation. The power of the Prophet Harris's god had allowed him to overcome successfully several of the Europeans' efforts to defeat him. Their prison cell could not hold him, and an official who mistreated him had died. And Harris wanted to share this power with the Ivorians.

That so many colonial officials from both the Gold Coast and the Ivory Coast had commented on Harris's effectiveness in making the Africans more diligent workers indicates that his impact on their work habits must have approached the magnitude of his influence on their religious behavior. His message provided them with a compelling reason to work.

Because the French had been trying to make the Ivorians work on their development projects, it appears at face value that the prophet was urging the Ivorians to play into the hands of the colonialists and to contribute more diligently to their own exploitation. However, the part of the message exhorting them to pray for seven years suggests another interpretation. Harris was telling the Ivorians that by acquiescing to the authority of the colonizers and learning their techniques, although they would initially be serving the foreigners' interests, within seven years they would be able to use these techniques to further their own interests and to regain their lost autonomy. They could learn to use the colonizers' means to attain their own ends. He was not urging their accommodation to the colonial reality, but was proposing a pragmatic plan to change it.

It is this interpretation of his leadership that made the prophet and the village churches built to perpetuate his teachings seem to the French to be such a threat. In addition, the interethnic unity he had provoked was also not in the interest of the colonizers, who recognized the difficulty they would have in trying to control a large group of Africans with the common goal of regaining their autonomy.

The Catholic missionaries' collusion with the colonial administration in trying to crush Harris's movement of indigenous Christian enthusiasm demonstrates how their religion functioned in the service of colonialism. Had their goal been to Christianize the Africans for the Africans' own good, they might have welcomed such expressions of enthusiastic indigenous Christianity among the people they were themselves inadequate to serve. But French Catholicism functioned as an arm of colonial control rather than as a superior spiritual force that would liberate the Ivorians from the abuses and limitations of their indigenous religion. Harris, in contrast, offered a Christian message that would free the Ivorians both from the spiritual constraints of their indigenous religion and from the oppression of the colonial system. This was why the French expelled him.

One may speculate about the reaction of Harris's Ivorian converts to the news of his expulsion. Because he was not a native of the

Ivory Coast and had made only brief stops in each place, leaving the country entirely for a while to go to the Gold Coast, he had set no precedent that would lead people to expect his continued presence. His technique had been to baptize people and leave them, telling them that others would come after him to instruct them further. He designated the clerk-disciples to act as his successors, and some of them were apparently assumed to be the prophet himself; so many people probably never knew of his expulsion. Furthermore, he had told people to join the Catholic church or to build their own churches, a direction suggesting that his purpose was to give his converts the impetus to be Christians and to play no further role in the process. Thus, Harris's departure, under whatever circumstances, was a perfectly normal event in his pattern of activities; the clerk-disciples continued his work; the Catholic missionaries were there to receive people; and in ten years, missionaries with Bibles did indeed arrive to teach his converts the Word of God.

CHAPTER 4

Aftermath and New Directions

The Movement after Harris (1915–1926)

After the Prophet Harris's expulsion from the Ivory Coast, his movement developed in several directions as his converts sought to practice the new religion correctly. Many people flocked to the Catholic mission churches. Others tried to continue worshiping as Harris had taught them, in some cases with the aid of his clerk-disciples, in others on their own, while awaiting the arrival of the teachers with Bibles. A further option developed for this group in 1924 when Protestant missionaries arrived and claimed to be the teachers whose coming Harris had foretold. An additional option was created when some people who had initially joined the Protestants subsequently became discontented and struck out on their own path, forming the nucleus of the Harrist Church of the Ivory Coast.

THE CATHOLICS

Like the Protestants in the Gold Coast, the Catholic missionaries in the Ivory Coast were obliged to increase their facilities to accommodate the great numbers of Harris's converts, for whom they were entirely unprepared, in view of their own unimpressive conversion record. Churches that had had ample space three years before Harris's coming had to be enlarged to accommodate the eager crowds who traveled long distances to the mission churches. Prior to Harris's arrival there were only a few hundred people being prepared for baptism by the Catholic missionaries; in

56

1917 there were eight thousand people who wanted to join their church; and in 1922 there were more than twenty thousand people eager to join.

The Catholic fathers recognized that Harris's great success resulted from an appeal to the Ivorians that they could not duplicate. Nevertheless, they were incapable of appreciating or respecting his methods because of their insensitive and ethnocentric disdain for anything African. Father Gorju said of the prophet: "What he did none of us would have been able to, indeed, because the methods were forbidden to us. That hallucinating man, who was also a charlatan, did, in barely three months, what we, ministers of Our Lord Jesus Christ, were not even able to begin doing in twenty years" (1917: 579). Nonetheless, even though they arrogantly denigrated the prophet and condemned his methods, the Catholic missionaries took full advantage of the fruits of his labors.

Although the Catholic missionaries were initially the only missionaries present, they did not succeed in attracting all of Harris's converts. Their insufficient numbers and facilities were factors limiting their ability to accommodate such large numbers.

There were also clear reasons why many people chose not to join the Catholic church. A most obvious one was that the Catholic church was intimately associated with the colonial administration that continued to cause the Ivorians so many hardships and to deprive them of their autonomy. Many people would not voluntarily give over to these same foreigners control over their spiritual lives as well.

Other people believed joining the Catholic church to be incompatible with Harris's teachings. A major element of his message was that the Word of God was contained in the Bible, and his own Bible was always very much in evidence. He emphasized that the Ivorians must learn to read so as to be able to learn God's will from the Bible. Thus many of his converts assumed that the Bible was an essential feature in the worship of Harris's god. Some of those who went to the Catholic church after Harris's expulsion, not finding the Bible in evidence, left again, concluding that the Catholic missionaries were not true Christians and were not the people by whom Harris would want them to be taught. In addition, the Catholic masses did not include the songs and processions that had been a part of the worship of Harris's god, and the services were in Latin, not the African languages in which Harris had told his converts to worship.

French support for the growth of the Catholic church came about as colonial officials became increasingly apprehensive about the tens of thousands of Harris's converts who called themselves "Harrist Protestants." The French associated this Protestant orientation with the influence of England, the neighboring and competing colonial power, and this association was exacerbated by the leadership role among the Harrist Protestants of the clerk-disciples from British colonies. Such foreign influence was particularly threatening at a period when the French, having defeated the Ivorians militarily, were trying to win their allegiance. Their fear of a British menace in this process was not entirely unfounded. Those Agni who found themselves on the Ivory Coast side of the colonial border with the Gold Coast felt that their Gold Coast relatives were better treated by the British, and some fled across the border to escape French domination.

The French colonial administration began to view the Catholic church as a strong ally against this undesirable foreign, Protestant influence. Consequently, colonial officers forced Harrist Protestants to relinquish to the Catholic missionaries the churches they had built for themselves. In 1921 it was decreed that all religious instruction and services in the colony must be in French, Latin, or the local Ivorian languages, a measure designed to decrease further the influence of Harris's English-speaking disciples.

In return for this government favor, the Catholic church increased its efforts to inculcate loyalty to France and to French culture as an integral part of the Christianity they taught to the Ivorians. The Catholic church and France were equated, as in a song the son of the patriarch of the Harrist church learned in Catholic school in the Ivory Coast, but found to be unknown to Catholics he met in France:

Heard from high in the heavens
The Church and the Nation
Catholic and French forever.

THE PROTESTANTS

Tens of thousands of Harrist Protestants. In many villages that Harris or his disciples had visited, or from which delegations had gone to see the prophet, the people, with or without assistance, practiced the new religion. Those who had been baptized by the prophet or one of his disciples provided the motivating force for the others. They prayed and sang the songs the prophet had taught them. They made up songs in their own languages and tried to observe the Sabbath and to follow the other rules of conduct that they considered to be Christian.

The Harrist Protestants built churches that were often the finest structures in their villages, some even being made of stone with tin roofs. They sometimes sent far to obtain materials and assistance for the construction of these churches. They usually had a bell near the entrance to call people to worship, and inside there were benches for the congregation. A table at the front of the church held the Bible. The minister stood behind the table; the apostles were seated on benches behind him. When the colonial administration set out to crush the Harrist movement, they gave the churches of highest-quality construction to the Catholic missionaries, burning or knocking down those that could be easily destroyed.

Although their churches were forbidden, many of the people who wanted to be faithful to Harris continued to worship in secret. Some dared to rebuild their churches, even at the risk of being imprisoned. They continued to pray and to wait for the people who, Harris had said, would come to teach them the contents of the Bible. A group of Harrist Protestants went to Grand Bassam to request that the Methodist church there, attended by clerks from the Gold Coast, find them a missionary, for the payment of which they had collected a large sum of money. The church leaders could not send them a missionary, however, so the people continued to worship and to wait, aware that they were not sure of the direction to take and hoping that someone would come along to lead them. Villagers from the Abidjan area sang the following song:

We are in the shadows
Our hope is on the sea
From which teachers will come to enlighten us
The word of Harris does not change. [Amos-Djoro 1956: 171]

A Protestant missionary from the Gold Coast quoted a letter describing the similar situation created there by Harris's activities:

Whereas it has pleased God Almighty, and His Spirit has moved us that we should no more bow down to any image or any kind of idol, I, as the Chief of Abura and its villages, with all my people have thrown away all our images, idols, charms and anything that we worshiped as our gods. We have also burnt all the temples of our gods which we first knew to be the guiders of the town. My people and I therefore appeal to your Church for a teacher who can manage the church and the school. . . . We are prepared to build up a church house to seat 300 people, because over 300 of us are very willing to serve God Almighty in the way you direct us. As we have appealed to you, we depend upon your Church to help to bring us to the salvation which the Lord has so freely directed us to. To avoid the devil visiting us any more, we pray that your Church supplies our need by sending a teacher here before the close of the month. [Armstrong 1920: 40–41]

The missionary then commented: "This letter was one of many received in those strenuous days. Deputations arrived daily from far distant unknown places for help, and the burden of the message was always the same: 'We have burnt our idols and charms, send us a teacher.' In a period of twelve months there were over fifty such appeals and about half of them were answered" (Armstrong 1920: 40–41).

Ironically, it was the French decree concerning the languages in which church services could be held, designed to eliminate the British Protestant influence, that brought Protestant missionaries into the colony to respond to the Harrist Protestants' desire for teachers. When, pursuant to this ruling, the French closed the Fanti Methodist church in Grand Bassam, Rev. William J. Platt, who was in charge of Methodist missionary work in Togo and Dahomey, came to the Ivory Coast to seek a remedy.

Upon arriving, Platt found many more Protestants than he had come to assist. A French lawyer he met in Grand Bassam told him that there were thousands of Africans in the area who called themselves Harrist Protestants, delegations of whom had asked him to find them teachers. He reproached Platt because the Protestants had not sent missionaries earlier to respond to this appeal.

Thus, whereas he had expected to find in the Ivory Coast a maximum of six thousand Gold Coast Protestants, Platt found tens of thousands of Ivorian Harrist Protestants who had built churches and were waiting for teachers. During his visits, in 1923 to see about reopening the Fanti church and in 1924 to begin providing missionaries for the Harrist Protestants, Platt visited an estimated forty villages and preached to more than eleven thousand people (Amos-Djoro 1956: 185; Bianquis 1924: 1151: Thompson 1928: 637).

In the numerous villages Platt visited, the reception was the same. The villagers turned out to meet him en masse, flocking to hear his words. They begged him to send them teachers. According to one Protestant missionary, villagers said things such as: "Dear missionary, we have made many mistakes since our Prophet left us because we are still very ignorant; ask God to pardon us; with your advice we will walk straight now" (Bianquis 1924: 1151). Another missionary was told by an old man, "We were blind and you have come to help us see. You must teach us how to serve God" (Bianquis 1924: 1154).

People in villages where he had expected to find no Christians at all told him that he had come just in time. They had been trying for a long time to remain faithful to Harris's teachings and to wait for the teachers he had said would come, but they were about to despair. The older men, the village leaders of the new religion, were trying to keep the fires of faith burning until the arrival of the teachers with Bibles. The young men, having no personal allegiance to Harris or his teachings, were eager to acquire the new skills taught by the Catholics in their mission schools, which would give them access to employment, financial independence, and material goods.

A Protestant missionary dramatically described the situation of one village in which the young men, feeling that the Catholics provided their only hope of getting an education, had decided to go to the Catholic church the following Sunday. As luck, or divine providence, would have it, Platt arrived in the village just before the chosen day, in time to rekindle their hope and to give them the impetus to await the arrival of the Protestant missionaries he promised would come.

Harris had said that young people should go to school to learn to read so that they could share the Word of God contained in the Bible with their elders. In the village of Tiassalé, sixty miles north of Dabou, the elderly Harrist minister who, with the aid of a Fanti clerk, was trying to maintain the religion of the prophet is reported to have told a Protestant missionary that if they would send one teacher, all of the people who had joined the Catholic church to learn to read the Bible would surely return to the Protestant fold. In another village, the older men had managed to remain true to Harris until 1937, when they finally had the opportunity to ask a Protestant missionary to send them a teacher before the prophet's religion died out entirely with the people who had known him (Bianquis 1924: 1152; Ching 1950: 125–26; F. Walker 1926: 60, 64).

When news of Platt's discovery of tens of thousands of Africans just waiting for Protestant missionaries to come to teach them reached missionary circles in England and France, a handful of missionaries was sent to respond to the call. Young Dahomean Protestants who knew something about the Bible were also recruited to help. They were minimally prepared to undertake such work, but were literate in French and added to the effort. Sixteen months after the Protestant missionaries began their work in the Ivory Coast, they had 160 congregations under their care. In the words of one missionary: "More the 32,000 people had their names on our church registers—illiterate people suddenly precipitating themselves into our arms, all needing to be taught, and eager to learn the first principles of the Gospel. *A mass movement? It is rather an avalanche! We have known nothing like it in our century and a half of missionary work*" (F. Walker 1926: 37; emphasis added).

The Protestants reopened the church at Grand Bassam and set up stations at Abidjan, Dabou, Grand Lahou, and Dimbokro in the interior, with a large concentration of Protestants in the area west of Grand Lahou (F. Walker 1926: 38). Because there were fewer than thirty missionaries and catechists, each person was responsible for providing services for many villages. They also held classes for ministers from the Harrist Protestant churches in villages having no missionary, to prepare them to return to their villages to teach (Platt 1934: 142–43).

By 1926 the colonial government permitted the Protestant missionaries to build a school at Dabou for the purpose of training young men as catechists. They were to learn the rudiments of

Christianity within one year and then to evangelize their own people. Developed to respond to the need created by the Prophet Harris's religious revolution, the school eventually became the Protestant seminary that continues to provide training for young Ivorian men entering the ministry (F. Walker 1926: 67).

The founder of the Protestant mission. Because of the reception they received from Harris's converts, the Protestant missionaries came to consider themselves his true successors. They compared his role to that of John the Baptist, who baptized people in preparation for their salvation by Jesus Christ. They believed that God had sent the prophet to prepare the way for themselves: "As we consider this strong man, with his devotion and his fanaticism, his limited grasp of the Truth, yet his earnestness in preaching what he knows, we can but thank God for him. We believe him to be a 'man sent by God' to the tribes of the Ivory Coast, and we rejoice that our beloved Missionary society has been called to carry on his work" (F. Walker 1927a: 141).

Thus the Protestant missionaries acknowledged Harris as the founder of the Protestant mission in the Ivory Coast. They divided the religious history of the Ivory Coast into three phases: (1) Harris's preaching; (2) the "ten years of waiting"—the period between Harris's departure and the arrival of the contingent of Protestant missionaries to continue his work; and (3) the establishment of the Protestant missions to gather in the people Harris had baptized. These developmental phases were as meaningful to the Ivorians who became Protestants as they were to the foreign missionaries. For those people who, after baptism by Harris, awaited teachers to instruct them, the arrival of the Protestant missionaries represented the fulfillment of the prophet's message.

Contemporary Ivorian Methodists acknowledge Harris as the founder of their church. In the village of Abobo-Doumé, a sign on the Protestant church building reads: "Protestant Wesleyan Mission —Founder William Wade Harris." The Methodist church celebrated its fiftieth year in the Ivory Coast in 1964, fifty years after the beginning of Harris's activity, not fifty years after the arrival of the Protestant missionaries. Ernest Amos-Djoro, an intellectual and a seminary-educated Ivorian Methodist, contends that the Methodists should more completely acknowledge Harris's key role in the founding of their mission in the Ivory Coast by naming their church the Wesleyan-Harrist Methodist church. To do so would provide clear acknowledgment of the Methodist debt to him (Amos-Djoro 1956: 355, 375).

The three paths. To be sure, because of his forceful and appealing message, his technique of presenting it, and the receptive audiences he found, William Wade Harris created a widespread situation of religious ferment in most of the southern Ivory Coast. He proved the indigenous religions to be inadequate in the face of the complex realities of the colonial situation, obliging his converts to choose among the various possible replacements he offered to them. The three options allowed by the prophet's message were joining the Catholic church, joining the Protestant church, and building their own churches.

Many people became Catholic because the Catholic missionaries were immediately present; others refrained because some Catholic practices did not correspond to the expectations Harris had created. Others became Protestant when the Methodist missionaries arrived because they believed them to be the prophet's rightful successors. Some people, having originally chosen the first or second option, subsequently changed their minds and created a third. This group concluded that none of the European missionaries were really practicing the religion of the Prophet Harris. They thus endeavored to perpetuate Harris's teachings as they understood them, with no foreign assistance. From this group developed the Harrist Church of the Ivory Coast, which claims to be the only institution that has faithfully implemented the prophet's message.

Two Visits, Two Mandates, Two Destinies (1926–1928)

In 1926, and again in 1928, Harris received in his home in Liberia visitors from the Ivory Coast seeking his guidance. Each of the visitors claimed exclusive rights to the prophet's mandate, and each was destined to determine the fate of large numbers of his converts. Stimulated by these visits, a controversy arose concerning Harris's real intentions: did he want to create a church, or did he merely intend to bring people to the knowledge of the Christian god in order to prepare them for salvation and education by the missionaries? Should there even be a Harrist church? The Protestants maintain that the Harrists are misled and that, according to the prophet's wishes, they should have joined the Protestant church. The Harrists counter that the Africans who are Protestant are untrue to the prophet and are not the African Christians he wanted them to be.

PIERRE BENOIT'S VISIT: THE FIRST MANDATE

When the Protestant missionaries arrived in the Ivory Coast at Platt's bidding, one of their first concerns was to find the Liberian prophet who had had such a radical influence on the large mass of Africans who claimed to be Harrist Protestants. In the words of Protestant missionary Jean Bianquis: "If Harris is still, at this time, in Sierra Leone,[1] it would be interesting for one of our missionaries, possessing a critical mind yet sympathetic to the blacks, [and] knowing well their religious psychology, to go question him about his memories, and to clear up the obscure points of this remarkable indigenous evangelization campaign in the Ivory Coast. It remains for us to see what have been its consequences during the past ten years" (1924: 1106).

Having ascertained that Harris was still alive in Liberia, the missionary Pierre Benoit, accompanied by African catechist Victor Tano (named after the river spirit), who had been baptized by Harris and who had interpreted for him, set out to find him. They spent the time from 22 September to 8 October 1926 in Graway and the vicinity, talking to the prophet and his family and to Protestant missionaries and other people who knew him (Amos-Djoro 1956: 199; Parrinder 1969: 151).

On the day Benoit set out to find Harris's home in Graway, he was surprised to see the prophet coming to meet him, dressed in his white garment and carrying his cross. Harris told him that several days earlier he had seen in a vision someone coming to visit him, and so he had set out to meet the person. The elderly prophet was overjoyed to receive news of the people he had converted in the Ivory Coast and was very eager to know what was becoming of them. According to Benoit's journal, Harris had tried unsuccessfully more than eight times since 1915 to reenter the Ivory Coast to finish the task he had begun (Amos-Djoro 1956: 210). He had hoped to be able to explain his mission to the colonial governor at Bingerville and to receive his permission to complete it (F. Walker 1927b: 111).

Harris had much to say about his converts. He emphasized repeatedly that the people in the Ivory Coast still had "fetishes" and were not worshiping the Christian god, and that the time was short. Someone had to teach them that they must change or be severely punished by God. He showed Benoit a Bible verse to convince him that God would soon send fire from heaven to burn the infidels who were worshiping the devil (F. Walker 1927b: 110). Benoit assured Harris that the Wesleyan Methodist Mission Society was continuing his mission, bringing the people he had baptized into the Protestant church for instruction. Harris was apparently impressed and pleased.

The prophet showed Benoit a copy of the *Christian Herald*, a Protestant missionary journal containing an article on Platt's first visit to the Ivory Coast, including photographs of both Platt and Harris. Harris was already aware, then, that Protestant missionaries had arrived to work with his converts. When Harris asked Benoit if he knew Platt, Benoit replied that he had come in Platt's name (Amos-Djoro 1956: 211).

Harris urged Benoit to recruit more missionaries to teach his converts, saying, "May missionaries and messengers be sent from everywhere" (F. Walker 1927b: 111–12). Apparently convinced that the Protestant missionaries were continuing the task he had begun, Harris dictated to Benoit a message for the people he had baptized:

MESSAGE FROM THE PROPHET WILLIAM WADE HARRIS TO
THE CHURCHES THAT I FOUNDED IN THE IVORY COAST

I, William Wade Harris, who called you to the truth of the Bible and baptism, have given this message to Pastor P. Benoit, so that he could bring it to you for you to obey. All the men, women and children who were called and baptized by me must enter the Methodist Church. No one must join the Roman Catholic Church if he wants to remain faithful to me. Mr. Platt, director of our Methodist Church, is designated by me as my successor at the head of the Churches that I founded.

All fetishes must be destroyed. Burn them all in the fire. May the Devil beset anyone who keeps them secretly in his house! May celestial fire devour them! Everyone must adore the only true God in Jesus Christ and serve Him alone!

Read the Bible, it is the Word of God. I am sending you one in which I have marked the verses that you should read. Seek the light in the Bible. It will be your Guide.

Be faithful in all things, practicing carefully the Ten Commandments and the Word of Jesus Christ, our only savior.

I send you my wishes and my message of joy. May God in his graciousness bless you abundantly.

Signed: W. W. Harris
      Cape Palmas
      25 September 1926
[Amos-Djoro 1956: 225]

The message was transcribed in French in two copies, one for Harris and one for Benoit. Harris affixed his two thumbprints, as well as his signature, and the nine witnesses present added their names or thumbprints (Amos-Djoro 1956: 225; F. Walker 1926: 174–75). Photographs of Harris and Benoit were taken, including two with Tano and members of Harris's family. A Protestant missionary in the Ivory Coast ten years later saw tears come to the eyes of the old men when he entered their villages for the first time, showed them copies of these photographs, and read them Harris's message (Roux 1971: 33).

Although the prophet's directive not to attend the Catholic church conflicted with his previous behavior and instructions, a knowledgeable and critical Ivorian intellectual who had known Benoit and read his journal believed Benoit's contention that the transcription was exact. He explained Harris's insistence that his converts become Protestant by the fact that the prophet was himself Protestant.

One must also consider the competitive, defensive, and sometimes hostile attitudes the Protestant and Catholic missionaries expressed toward one another, as exhibited by Gorju's statement about the "Protestant conspiracy." A major reason for Benoit's visit, furthermore, was to identify the prophet with the Protestants in order to give them legitimacy in the eyes of his converts. Benoit could have gained the prophet's favor very easily by accurately describing the Catholic church's collaboration with the colonial administration in persecuting Harris's followers for their efforts to be Christians.

Because of the prophet's concern that his converts continue along the path in which he had begun to lead them, it was neither surprising nor inconsistent for him to have indicated a preference for the missionary efforts of the Protestants, who had attributed sufficient importance to his impact on the Ivorian people to send a representative to seek his advice. Harris might just as easily have shifted his flock in favor of Catholicism had he been approached by the Catholics. He had said that he was preparing his converts to be taught by "Catholic and Protestant men of God," and whereas he had led them to Protestant churches in the Gold Coast, in the Ivory Coast he led them to the Catholics. His intention was simply to help the Africans to become Christians. Like Blyden, he considered the denominational schisms created in Europe irrelevant in Africa.

Unlike the Protestants, the Catholics made no special effort to establish themselves as the prophet's successors, although they had swelled their numbers with his converts when they were the only missionaries present. Furthermore, the French colonial administration had begun to give increasing support to the Catholics because of their contribution to the overall colonial effort to make the Ivorians acquiescent to French domination. The Protestants, therefore, had a definite interest in creating an advantage for themselves with the Ivorian populations by associating themselves with the Liberian prophet whose work they had specifically come to continue.

Upon Benoit's return from Liberia, the Protestant mission made public the contents of Harris's message. Those Ivorians who, seeking to comply with Harris's desires, had previously hesitated to join the Methodist church now joined in large numbers, increasing its enrollment to three times the size of the Catholic mission (Amos-Djoro 1956: 216). Many people who had become Catholic when there was no Protestant mission changed allegiance. After Harris's death in fall 1929, the Protestants hung in their churches copies of the photograph of Harris and Benoit, with Harris's message to his converts directing them to the Protestant mission (Grivot 1942: 88).

JOHN AHUI'S VISIT:
THE SECOND MANDATE

Instead of securing the position of the Protestant missionaries as Harris's only legitimate successors, the message brought by Benoit instead provoked a dispute concerning its authenticity. The major disputants were not among those persons who sided with the Catholic cause, as might have been anticipated. The problem lay elsewhere: instead of convincing all those baptized by Harris that they should become Protestant, the message stimulated some Ivorians, dissatisfied with the Protestant missionaries and suspicious of the document, to wish to visit Harris personally.

The people of Petit Bassam, after having been baptized by the Prophet Harris in Bingerville, built a church in their village. The villagers were all Harrist Protestants for ten years under the guidance of Chief Akadja Nandjui, until a schism developed in reaction to the newly arrived Methodist missionaries. Whereas the villagers had initially received the missionaries with equal enthusiasm, one faction became disaffected as the missionaries sought to deprive indigenous church leaders of their autonomy and demanded unacceptable changes in social practice. This schism provided the impetus for the formation of a second delegation to visit Harris, this time representing the Harrist Protestants themselves.

After Benoit's visit, according to some Harrists, the Protestants told the Ivorians that Harris was dead. Another former interpreter of Harris's, named Dougbo, suggested to Chief Nandjui that a delegation be sent to verify whether the prophet was dead or alive. Accordingly, in 1928, Dougbo, John Ahui (the chief's son and the leader of the chorus that sang for religious ceremonies), and Ahui's uncle, Solomon Dagri, set off to Liberia to see if Harris was still alive. If he was, they were to ask him if Benoit's message really expressed his desires and if the Methodist missionaries were actually implementing his teaching as he wished.

Some Harrists contend that Harris told the Ivorian delegation that Benoit had deceived him and that the message was false. According to this claim, Benoit had led Harris to believe that the Protestants were helping his converts to worship as he had taught, although they were not really doing so. These Harrists also maintain that the prophet told the Ivorian delegation that he had not given the Protestants his mandate to take up his work and to gather in his converts; on the contrary, he wanted his followers to remain true to him by worshiping on their own as he had taught them.

It is ironic that the Protestants' effort to establish themselves as Harris's only true successors had the unanticipated effect of stimulating rather than quelling the Ivorian quest for spiritual autonomy. If the Protestants falsely told the Ivorians that the Prophet Harris was dead, it was to establish themselves as the final authority about his intentions, and to discourage them from seeking justification for any course of action other than joining the Protestant mission. That this effort to forestall the Ivorians' desire for religious autonomy instead precipitated it is doubly ironic, considering that the French effort to destroy the autonomous Harrist movement had directly provoked the arrival of the Protestants. Thus both European efforts to eliminate expressions of African religious freedom had the unintentional effect of contributing to their growth.

The Ivorian delegation complained to Harris that the Protestants had made unacceptable demands on them as the condition for allowing them to join the church. They said that the Protestants demanded "tickets" (cards given to parishioners when they paid quarterly tithes) to perform baptisms, and added that the missionaries would not admit them to the church if they maintained more than one wife. Harris had neither accepted money for his baptism nor said that men should be monogamous. The effect of the Protestant prohibition of polygamy was that those men most highly respected in the indigenous society for their wealth and power, a visible manifestation of which was their many wives and children, were forbidden to attend church by the foreigners who claimed to be the prophet's successors. This missionary exigency was, to the Ivorians, a blatant violation of Harris's respect for the indigenous social system.

Just as he had done for Benoit, Harris provided his Ivorian visitors with a written message, in this case entitled his "Last Will and Testament" addressed to the people he had baptized, answering the questions posed by the three men and providing direction for the religious life of his converts. The text is as follows:

THE LAST WILL AND TESTAMENT
OF THE PROPHET HARRIS GIVEN TO JOHN AHUI, 1928

Part One

I, Prophet [was] sent to preach in the kingdom of Adjah
Nandjui, Petit Bassam, Ivory Coast.

The Prophet wants to come back, but God does not want him
to.

France is making war on the king of Ethiopia and on his subjects. Let no Black man go to Europe.[2]

The French used physical violence against the Prophet; for this
reason their Motherland "La Belle France" will be terribly
shaken.

The Prophet bids you farewell. He is ready to go to the Celestial Home. See chapter 4.[3] Remember the law of Moses, the
servant of God.

The conference of peace is the conference of war, says the
Prophet. The Liberian Kru coast is lost.[4] Read Isaiah, chapter 4.[5]
Read the Gospel According to Saint Mark, Chapter 10.[6]

John Dibo[7]   William Wade Harris[8]
   (his X)   (his X)

Part Two

Among the pagan people whom we try to lead in the path of
God, we do not receive tickets either for baptism, or for confirmation.

How can we expect to receive blessings from God if we have
already received our payment here below.

Those who collect money for themselves are false prophets.

In the house of God, in the middle of the people whom we are
trying to lead in the path of God, we do not receive tickets, nor
do we sell them [any more] for baptism than for confirmation.

Dear Christians do not let anyone fool you.

You must always courageously keep your morale high like old
Saint Paul or like Socrates.

If you say that you are for God, you must suffer many tribu-
lations without abandoning God for all that.

I will always remember you to God in my prayers.

The Prophet sends you[9] his greetings in the name of God, the God of Moses, Isaac, and Jacob.

I am full of pride to see the spiritual force and courage that you have demonstrated in the name of God in sending your son and your brother to see me here in Liberia.

May God bless you in the same way.

I will always think of you in my prayers, and [of] all of the Christians in Ivory Coast as well.

You must always keep God in mind. It is He who will save you from all temptation.

Do not leave your God to save your life.

I am now old and often sick. God tells me to stay at home to await my time; it may be sooner or later.[10]

We do not pay anything for our religion. Here in Liberia we receive baptism and confirmation free.

I hope that you respect Sunday, the Holy Day of God.

May God bless you.

I am Yours in Christ.

Marie Agre   William Wade Harris

Part Three

Again I say to you in the name of God that if you marry two women, that is awkward, but do it if you can not do otherwise.

One thing, however: you must follow your God.

Do not let anyone fool you

If you can marry ten women, do it, but follow the rules of God.

William Wade Harris
[Amos-Djoro 1956: 225–28]

Remembering earlier persecution by both Catholic missionaries and the colonial administration, when other Harrist Protestants had tried to worship independently, and fearing reprisals this time from the Protestant missionaries, the Ivorian delegates did not make public the message the prophet had given them. Instead, they kept it at the church headquarters in Petit Bassam, consulting it privately as the basis for their efforts to follow Harris's directives.

In response to the delegation's description of what they considered to be abusive practices of the Protestant missionaries,

Harris had urged his converts not to let themselves be fooled by anyone. He knew, the Harrists contend, that the Protestants were more concerned with their own interests and the extension of their influence than with bringing benefits to the Africans. Therefore, the Harrists maintain, the prophet wanted them to pursue their own interests independently and not let the Europeans take advantage of them. This was not an unreasonable warning from the prophet in view of the physical violence the French had used against him when he undertook to fulfill his divine mission.

Harrist tradition has it that while the three Ivorians were in Liberia, the prophet gave them a test as a basis for deciding which of them should succeed him. He told each man to look into the sun, where he would see a human form. The two older men looked and said that they saw the form, but John Ahui stated that he was unable to see it. For his honesty, Ahui was chosen by the prophet as his successor (Yando 1970: 67). Harris gave him a Bible and a large cross like the one he himself carried.

Thus, John Ahui came to be considered the prophet's spiritual heir and the leader of the nascent Harrist church. Ahui, Dagri, and Dougbo were, like Benoit, photographed with Harris as proof that they had indeed visited him. The Harrists composed a song commemorating this event:

John Ahui went to visit Harris;
Harris gave him the holy commandments;
Before the return of John Ahui,
Harris, forewarned of the incredulity of people,
Had a photograph taken with John Ahui
In order to reassure the hesitant Africans.

THE TWO MANDATES

Each of the two visits and consequent mandates served its purpose. The Protestants gathered in many of the people baptized by Harris, and those who preferred to remain independent of the foreign missionaries also had direct justification from the prophet for doing so. On the basis of existing evidence it is impossible to prove whether one or the other of the two messages was apocryphal, but given the prevailing circumstances it is quite possible that both were valid.

When Benoit visited him, Harris was worried about the unfinished work he had left in the Ivory Coast. He repeatedly insisted that time was growing short and that people in the Ivory Coast were still practicing their indigenous religions. He was happy to hear that the missionaries had arrived to continue his work, and was aware of his converts' enthusiastic response to their arrival. Benoit told him that the Protestants were teaching people and bringing them into the church, which was Harris's great hope. Given that the preachers and teachers whose coming he had promised had arrived and were said to be doing what he had expected them to do, it was entirely consistent for Harris to give the Protestants his blessings to continue his work.

That Harris may have fully supported the Protestant missionaries in carrying on his work in no way invalidates his subsequent mandate to John Ahui. Ahui, Dagri, and Dougbo arrived with stories of mistreatment at the hands of the Protestant missionaries. In light of their grievances, the issue that they raised with the prophet was undoubtedly not whether they should join the Protestants, but rather whether they should keep or abandon the religion that Harris had brought them.

Seeking justification for refusing to join an institution they found oppressive, the Ivorian delegation would not have portrayed the Protestant mission in the most favorable light. Having found the awaited missionaries a severe disappointment, and wanting to follow Harris's teachings faithfully, they sought an alternative to the Protestant path.

Harris's great fear had been that his converts would revert to the old religious practices that he had convinced them to abandon. When the Ivorian delegates told him they had been practicing his religion as he had taught them, it was perfectly consistent for the prophet to urge them to continue worshiping as they had been doing before the arrival of the Protestants. Because of his advanced age, and because of what he believed to be the magnitude and urgency of his task, he continued to seek assistance in fulfilling his divine mission, just as he had done in the Ivory Coast when he delegated disciples to help him spread his message of salvation.

A final element to consider is that when Benoit went to see Harris, the only options that he would have cited were for the prophet's converts to become Protestant or Catholic, or to return to the indigenous religion. Because he was pleased with Benoit's visit, it was clearly appropriate for Harris to affirm the work of the Protestants. The Ivorian delegation offered another option likely to assure that even larger numbers of his converts would remain Christian.

The Prophet's True Intentions

It was noted earlier that both Benoit and Ahui had their photographs taken with Harris. This photographic evidence added to the validity of each man's claim to being the rightful heir to Harris's ministry. The photograph in which Ahui is shown with Harris is a group photograph of the two men along with Dougbo, Dagri, and members of Harris's family. There is a similar picture of Pierre Benoit with Victor Tano and members of Harris's family, but Benoit is also pictured separately in another photograph, shaking hands with Harris. There is no similar photograph of Harris and Ahui. The Harrists have, however, resorted to a bit of photographic artistry and created a picture that symbolically illustrates their view of Ahui as Harris's only legitimate successor.

Using the photograph of Benoit and Harris, the Harrists removed the image of Benoit and replaced it with an image of Ahui, positioned so that it looks as if Harris is handing his cross, the symbol of his mission, to Ahui his successor. The montage is constructed very skillfully and might be mistaken for a genuine photograph except that Ahui appears as the elderly man he is now, rather than as the young man he was when he visited Harris decades ago.

The Harrists' understanding of Ahui's message from Harris was that it countermanded Benoit's, giving the Ivorians the responsibility and authority for taking charge of and unifying the entire movement begun by Harris. As their photographic image indicates, the Harrists believe that Ahui's mandate superseded Benoit's. It was on the basis of this position that Ahui established his version of the religion taught by Harris more than a decade after any Ivorian had last seen him. He and his two companions were the last Ivorians to see the prophet before his death. Whereas Harris had given Benoit a message to his converts, he presented to the Ivorian delegation his

"Last Will and Testament." Ahui thus became Harris's final and most authoritative disciple.

Ahui visited the prophet at a time when the movement Harris had begun had reached a point of indecision. Were those people who had tried to remain faithful to him to join the Protestant church, about which many people had reservations; or were they to take a new direction, and if so, which one? Ahui's mandate from the prophet in response to such questions provided the basis for his claim to orthodoxy. He took his mandate to mean that he was Harris's sole successor for the fulfillment of the prophet's mission. Accordingly, the church that Ahui established is based, in its organizational structure and doctrinal content, as closely as possible on Harris's teachings.

Although Harrists and Protestants get along perfectly well on the concrete level of everyday life, there are fundamental conflicts on the level of church doctrine. The official Harrist stance is to challenge the Protestants' claims to the allegiance of any of Harris's converts because the prophet recognized that the foreign missionaries were not working for the Ivorians' interests. Protestants simply deny that there should exist a Harrist church, basing their position on the claim that Harris had not intended to found a church. They contend that Harris had only wanted to baptize people, teach them the Word of God, and convince them to abandon their traditional religious practices. His converts were then to go to the existing Catholic churches or—more important to the Protestant argument —to wait for the teachers with Bibles to lead them.

Because Harris had told his converts to build churches where there were none, however, and to structure them with twelve apostles and a minister, and to say prayers and to sing songs in their own language, he did in effect encourage the Ivorians to create their own new religious institutions. He implicitly recognized this in the message he gave to Benoit, when he stated: "Mr. Platt, director of the Methodist church, is designated by me as my successor at the head of the *churches that I founded*" (emphasis added).

Harris's statements and actions indicate that he perceived his role as that of a prophet, paving the way for both Catholic and Protestant missionaries. Deliberately or not, however, he did provide the impetus and authority for the founding of an autonomous indigenous church. The message he shared with the Ivorians was unique.

The European missionary churches provided variants of this message, but their versions of Christianity did not contain the indigenous cultural elements and the prescription for regaining their lost sovereignty that the Ivorians found most attractive.

The key to the question whether there should really be a Harrist church distinct from the Protestant churches lies in the two visits. It is consistent with Harris's fervor about saving people before it was too late, and with his evident pragmatic orientation, to conclude that he intended for both Benoit and Ahui to continue what he clearly saw as a crucial task of great magnitude. The Protestants and Harrists each claim, for purely self-interested reasons, that their message from Harris was the only valid one. In doing so, both groups ignore the true meaning and intent of the prophet's mission.

Harris was a prophet whose revealed mission was to bring people to the Christian god. Mundane institutional antagonisms among Catholics, Protestants, and even Harrists did not concern him. Any church was good to the extent that it led people away from their indigenous religions and toward the knowledge and worship of the Christian god. Therefore, although Harris did not set out to establish a Harrist church, to the extent that the church fulfills the function of bringing people to the Christian god, its existence is consistent with his teachings.

He told his converts to go to the churches that were available, and where there were none, to build them. It follows that if people were dissatisfied with the missionary churches and were considering returning to their former beliefs and practices, Harris would have wanted them to create their own churches in which to worship his god. Thus, he both passed his mandate on to the Protestant mission to continue his work and delegated John Ahui to instruct his converts to continue worshiping as he had taught.

Essentially, the prophet charged Benoit and Ahui with different tasks. This difference was manifested in the ways in which he passed on his legacy to the two men. Harris's first message empowered the Protestant mission to gather in all of the people he had converted in order to teach them about Christianity. They were to carry to the next phase the process that he had begun. Harris's mandate to Benoit and the Protestant missionaries focused on the consolidation of the gains that had been made and the provision of spiritual and intellectual continuity.

Harris's delegation of responsibility to Ahui was different from, but not in conflict with, the legacy he left to the Protestant mission. To Ahui he gave the principal accoutrements of his role as prophet —the awe-provoking cane-cross he had used in conversions and a Bible. The meaning here is that, whereas he wanted the Protestants to provide a Christian education for the people he had converted, he wanted Ahui to continue his actual task of transforming worshipers of the indigenous spirits into worshipers of the Christian god. The two mandates actually delegated to each man the task for which he was most suited. Harris's own experience had already proven that an African could convince Africans to make a radical religious change more easily than a foreign missionary could ever hope to do. The missionaries, however, were better prepared to teach the contents of the Bible.

Thus, Ahui became Harris's spiritual successor, with the mission of taking up the cane-cross and going into the areas in which people had not yet been baptized, bearing the prophet's message. At this point, the significance of the test the Harrists say was given the three men becomes clearer. It was through a vision that Harris received his call to become a messenger of God; and a kind of vision was likewise employed to establish Ahui's suitability to succeed the prophet. Interestingly, in Ahui's case what was tested was not his spiritual ability, but rather his honesty.

Furthermore, although Harris may not have specifically intended for Ahui to establish a new church, his doing so was a logical consequence of his attempt to continue the prophet's mission. Given his disaffection with the Protestants, and the reality of Catholic oppression of the Harrist Protestants, it would have been inconsistent for Ahui to baptize people and to send them to either missionary church. Harris had taught his converts to worship using familiar indigenous forms, a practice radically different from the missionary style. As a result, to be true to his teachings, many of those converts institutionalized those indigenous forms in the Harrist Church of the Ivory Coast.

PART 2

The Creation of the

Harrist Church

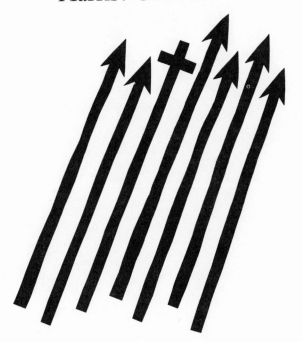

CHAPTER 5

Gathering in Harris's Converts

In the Prophet's Footsteps

The example of the Harrist leaders who had been persecuted and imprisoned by colonial administrators dissuaded the
members of the Ivorian delegation from beginning their missionary
work immediately on their return from Liberia. Some villagers,
however, believed that Solomon Dagri's death in 1931 was divine
punishment for his failure to aid his nephew in beginning to pursue
his religious duty. Thus, following his uncle's death, young John
Ahui set aside the villagers' fears for his life and began to spread the
news of Harris's Last Will and Testament, using the prophet's own
techniques for reaching people. He traveled on foot or by canoe,
sometimes alone because others were afraid to accompany him,
sometimes with a group of singers from his village. Ahui was assisted in his efforts by a few other courageous Ebrié men who were
determined to remain faithful to Harris.

One of Ahui's helpers was Noé Tché-Tché, first Harrist minister
of the village of Abobo-té, who insisted that he would not give up
his religion and was imprisoned for a time in Grand Bassam for his
conviction. The Harrist church in Abobo-té was destroyed several
times by the colonial guards, each time being rebuilt by faithful
Harrists under Tché-Tché's leadership. Tché-Tché was entrusted
with the task of ministering to the Ebrié villagers in the forest
northwest of the lagoons, and to the ethnic groups further inland.
Peter Loba, of the village of M'Badon, who had been given a cane-
cross by Harris in Bingerville, was given charge of the villages
northeast of the lagoons toward the Gold Coast. Ahui's area of
proselytizing was primarily the coastal strip between the lagoons
and the sea.

The ministers were often not well received in the villages they visited because colonial administrators warned the chiefs against welcoming them. In these cases, villagers refused to listen to them and even to extend customary hospitality. Harrists tell, however, of Ahui's success in spite of such adversity. According to one Harrist, for example, Ahui was walking one day on a road near Dabou, when suddenly a colonial commander stopped him at gunpoint and accused him of inciting people not to work. (The incident took place during the period of forced labor that lasted until 1945, during which time the French used whips to keep the Africans working.) The commander forbade the chief of the nearby village that Ahui was approaching to receive him. As a result, the chief, familiar with colonial force but not with the power of Ahui's god, would not extend to Ahui even the normal courtesy of asking him to sit down. He did offer the customary greeting, however, by asking him for the "news." Ahui told him that he had come to bring the word of his god. At this the chief, fearing punishment from the French, asked Ahui to leave the village.

As he departed, Ahui prayed to God as he knew Harris would have done, telling him that he had tried his best. Shortly thereafter, representatives of that very village went to see Ahui in Petit Bassam to ask how they could become Harrists. He received them warmly and welcomed them to the fold, baptizing them and instructing them in how to create their own Harrist church.

That spectacular conversions have been attributed to Ahui, just as they were to Harris, illustrates the Harrists' belief that Ahui did indeed inherit the prophet's spiritual power. One Harrist told of the time that Ahui had gone to the Sassandra area on foot, stopping in different villages to preach as Harris had done. Ahui tried to preach in one village in the area, but left because the residents would not listen to him. The next day, although it was sunny in other nearby villages, this village alone found itself in total darkness. The villagers sent a messenger to find Ahui, and all became Harrists.

Another Harrist told of an occasion when Ahui went to a village where a funeral was being celebrated and where the people would not listen to him. Upon leaving the village, he began to pray. When he finished praying, the dead woman suddenly sneezed, sat up, and asked what all of the people were doing around her. Needless to say, the villagers immediately called Ahui back to teach them about his god.

Ahui went to preach in another village in which the inhabitants wanted to have more children, but in which few were born. He told the villagers to pray as he instructed and to put one bean in a bag for each child born during the year. At the end of the year there were 120 beans, a number so far above the yearly norm that he easily converted most of those villagers who had initially refused to heed his teachings.

Another Harrist told of an inland village in which, ten years after having adopted the religion of the prophet, the villagers had returned to their indigenous religion. There was a river inhabited by spirits that the villagers did not dare to cross. When Ahui visited the village, he and the group of Harrists who accompanied him went to the river. They sang songs, prayed, and then walked into the taboo water—emerging unharmed. This "miracle" impressed the local people. They immediately wanted to be rebaptized by the "fighter of evil spirits," whose conversions diminished the enrollment of local missionary churches.

In spite of such spectacular conversions, however, the degree of control exercised over the lives of the Ivorians by the colonial administration prohibited Ahui and his assistants from achieving large-scale success in rekindling the fires of the Harrist movement.

The Nationalist Awakening

With the advent of the nationalist period in the 1940s, interest in practicing the religion of the prophet was reawakened. Because of the new political currents and diminished religious persecution, the Ivorians could now worship openly as they chose. Harrist churches began springing up in the coastal villages where memories of Harris's teachings had been preserved for three decades. People who had been baptized by Harris left the missionary churches en masse to join or to establish Harrist churches.

Although the incipient Harrist church never developed formal institutional links with the political nationalists, the two types of organizations—political and religious—were parallel in their determination to affirm their rejection of the imposition of European institutions and values. Some educated young people joined the Harrist church because it was an African church, and therefore consistent with their nationalist ideology; and some leading Harrists of today played important roles in the nationalist movement.

The nationalist period marked the beginning of the growth of the Harrist church as a significant institution. Before 1946, in the Abidjan area over which Ahui presided, there were three Harrist churches; after 1946, twenty-one new ones developed. Ahui and his assistants also increased their influence beyond the confines of the Ebrié area to other ethnic groups who had had contact with Harris, but with whom the Harrist ministers' own contacts had been limited by colonial authorities (Amos-Djoro 1956: 239).

During this time there were important mass conversions, the Ebrié village of Abobo-Doumé providing a pertinent example. The Harrist church in Abobo-Doumé dates to January 1948. Prior to this conversion, an estimated 98 percent of the villagers had been Catholic; the other 2 percent were Protestant.

According to the resident of Abobo-Doumé who described the conversion, many villagers preferred to spend their Sundays socializing and drinking palm wine, not going to mass. The Catholic priest in charge of the village tried to coerce them into attending mass more often by going to their houses to insist that they attend church, and reporting to the French commander that they cut down palm trees to make wine. He also forbade them to fish on Sunday, even though they needed fish to sell on Monday. The priest even had colonial guards sent to break up the Sunday festivities of the people not at mass. The village chief helped the French persecute the villagers, who were frequently compelled to perform forced labor, such as working on road construction gangs, for the week after they failed to attend mass.

The villagers, particularly irate about the chief's collusion with the French, resolved to tolerate this treatment no longer. Not feeling that they could rid themselves of the chief, because the colonial authorities backed him, they decided to change their religious affiliation. With the support of some of the elders who also disagreed with the chief, a delegation of villagers visited Petit Bassam to tell Ahui that they wanted to establish a Harrist church. When Ahui reminded them that attempts had been made in the past to get them to practice Harris's religion, they said that they were now ready and that there would be a great many converts. The old people who had seen the Prophet Harris were pleased to be able to return to a church in which they could worship in a way satisfying to them and in which the coercion associated with the missionary churches was absent.

The atmosphere of the Harrist religious services was jubilant. The new converts created their own songs and sang them to the rhythms of their gourd rattles in gay processions up and down the main street of the village. According to one Harrist minister, "When the Harrist church came to Abobo-Doumé on 29 January 1948 everyone was joyful." Why? "Because before the Harrist mission came to this village, we lived in a state of doubt. People were Catholic or Protestant, but they ran after fetishism."

In another village near Abidjan, the elders all decided to become Harrists as a protest against the missionaries who wanted to impose on them a priest they did not like. In 1949, in an Attié village, the Catholic priest told the villagers to put a group of visiting Harrists out of the village after the Harrists held a joyous procession that distracted people from the Catholic mass; the Catholic villagers replied that the Harrists were Africans like themselves, and rather than putting them out, many villagers joined them. Another Harrist reported that in 1946 in the village of M'Badon, in which everyone had traditionally belonged to the Harrist church, one person decided to become Catholic. On the day of his confirmation, he died, thus reinforcing the other villagers' faith in the Harrist church.

In some situations, however, in which the Harrist religion had not provided tangible proofs of its power, people eventually abandoned it just as they had forsaken previous religious forms when they proved inadequate. During the year after the residents of a village near Aboisso became Harrists, they suffered both many deaths in the village and a poor harvest. At the end of the year they decided to return to their traditional practices and to evacuate the village in which conditions were so bad.

The period of massive reconversion and reestablishment of Harrist churches lasted until about 1951. Since that time, membership has continued to spread geographically and to encompass more people from different ethnic groups, particularly since the Ivory Coast gained its independence in 1960.

Institutionalizing the Church

In August 1955 the first Harrist conference, composed of ministers, apostles, elders, and delegates from various Harrist churches, was held in Petit Bassam to reflect upon the historical evolution of the church and to make plans for its future (Amos-Djoro 1956: 240). This conference marked the culmination of the period, beginning with the nationalist impetus, during which the Harrist movement developed into the Harrist church. Conference participants praised John Ahui for competently directing the affairs of the church and for continuing to carry on the Prophet Harris's proselytizing mission with great courage and dedication. They began the effort to unite under his unitary leadership all of the people who claimed allegiance to Harris.

Pleased with their growing numbers, as the church obtained converts from both the missionary churches and the indigenous religion, conference participants discussed the possibility of spreading the Harrist church to other regions of the country and even beyond the limits of the Ivory Coast. In order to do so they felt that they would need to acquire a stable financial base, encourage more young people to be active in the church, and increase the level of schooling among the young. The most important proposals of the conference included:

> Choosing a motto: God, Work, Love, and Country;
>
> Creating the Young Harrist Movement: it was to be analogous to the scouts, with counterparts for boys and girls. Its role would be to perpetuate Harrist ideals of justice and love for humankind among young people so as to develop their natural virtues;
>
> Deciding to ask the government for funds to build a school;
>
> Establishing annual celebrations;
>
> Making decisions concerning the songs to be sung in church;
>
> Dividing the territory into districts under the jurisdiction of the Archbishop, the Bishop, the Cardinals, the Sacred College.
> [Amos-Djoro 1956: 240, 242]

It was at this conference that the decision was made to begin to codify the doctrine of the Harrist church. Bruno Claver, at that time a university student in Europe who had left the Catholic church to join the Harrists, was selected to edit the first official document.

The *Premier livret de l'education religieuse à l'usage des missions Harristes* (First booklet of religious education for the use of Harrist missions) was published on 1 August 1956. The intent of the booklet was to provide a common standard of knowledge to be used to inform church members. Unfortunately, the document was not disseminated and used as intended. A number of Harrists reported having heard of its existence, but never having seen it; others had never even heard of it. One young man from Petit Bassam said that the booklet had been much publicized in the church there. His family had bought a number of copies, and he had had one while in secondary school.

A brief discussion of the *Premier livret* is useful as an indication of the intentions of church leaders, even though it did not have the desired educational effect. It did represent, however, the first attempt to record and synthesize what had until then been a purely oral tradition. The twenty-three-page booklet, in question-and-answer form (it is sometimes referred to as the Harrist "catechism"), is divided into four chapters: "On Religions," "On the Community," "On the Acts," and "On the Commandments of the Harrist Church."

The first chapter, "On Religions," begins by saying that God sent each people its own prophet to reveal its religion to them. It relates how the Prophet Harris was called to become a prophet, speaks of his visit to the Ivory Coast, and outlines the organizational structure of the church. This chapter also indicates the reasons why people must not represent spiritual beings in material form:

> Q. What is God like?
> A. No one has ever seen him and no one ever will see God. It is for this reason that one must never worship God through a picture or a statue.
> Q. What does the person who bows before a picture or a statue representing God or a saint do?
> A. That person is committing idolatry because he is worshiping an object. God is pure spirit.
> Q. May one make a representation of God?
> A. No.
> Q. Why?
> A. Because no one has ever seen or ever will see God. God is

pure spirit. . . . To make a material representation of God, whatever may be the intention, is a diabolical practice. [Pp. 1–6]

The chapter "On the Community" begins with the biblical explanation of God's creation of the world in six days and then addresses the issue of correct social interaction, including the delineation of the responsibilities of family members and of employers and employees to each other. It says that God commands humans to marry in order to procreate and to perpetuate the species. A man may have several wives provided that he treats them and their children equally, and parents must provide schooling for their children. Family solidarity is stressed, as is love for non-kin. Although people are urged to be charitable, they are not to encourage beggars or parasitic individuals because laziness is a sin, whereas work brings people closer to God (pp. 7–12).

Chapter three, "On the Acts," describes church sacraments that are intended to assure human salvation. Baptism, the most important for the Harrists, follows the model established by the Prophet Harris:

The Preacher invites the postulant to kneel, to hold the holy cane-cross with his two hands. He puts the Holy Book on his head, saying: "This is the book of God; you must obey it." Then, having removed the Holy Book, the Preacher sprinkles water contained in a small receptacle on the person's head, in the name of the Father, the Son, and the Holy Ghost. If there are several people to baptize, the Preacher proceeds by groups, as the Prophet himself taught.

To receive baptism, one must be pure, renounce one's past sinful life, and be ready to learn to be a good Harrist. Babies may be baptized at their parents' request as protection until they are old enough for a definitive baptism. [Pp. 13–20]

The Harrist Commandments are listed in chapter four:

You will worship God alone.
You will love God by loving your neighbor.
You will not take the name of God in vain.
You will hate idolatry.
On Sunday, all work will be prohibited.
You will honor your father and mother.

You will not commit adultery.
You will not kill.
You will not steal.
You will not drink alcohol. [P. 21]

The *Premier livret*, published more than four decades after the Prophet Harris's momentous visit to the Ivory Coast, is a composite of the history and teachings of the prophet as contained in the oral tradition and in the will that Harris gave to John Ahui. It also includes biblical elements and remnants of Catholicism, because Claver and many other Harrist converts had received their prior religious education in the Catholic church. The booklet was intended to extend and to complete Harris's teachings, and to help the Harrists to adapt those teachings to contemporary life. Just as Harris provided social teachings relevant to the context into which he came, the *Premier livret* offered social teachings applicable to contemporary problems and conducive to the spirit of development that church leaders hoped to inspire in their members.

Harris, for example, urged his converts to work hard on every day but Sunday, and he personally played an important role during the colonial period in inspiring his converts to be diligent workers. The *Premier livret* continued this theme by saying that every person must work and that laziness is a sin. As the booklet recognized, the Harrist church would have to inculcate the work ethic in its members if it was to continue to thrive and to adapt to the rapid changes of contemporary Ivorian society. This emphasis on the value of work as a way of pleasing God may be viewed as an attempt to give work a spiritual significance going beyond its obvious pragmatic value.

In addition to the writing of the *Premier livret*, several proposals made at the 1955 conference were also implemented. The Harrists built a school in the Adjamé area of Abidjan, which today functions as a regular government school. The building of this school represented a step toward the fulfillment of an important aspect of the prophet's message—to provide schooling for children so that they could learn to read and thus convey the Word of God contained in the Bible to their elders.

Annual celebrations were established: the 27 July celebration is known as the Rain Feast, and 3 December is the Celebration of John

Ahui. Certain important Harrist villages have their own major celebrations, like the All Saints' Day celebration in Bregbo and the New Year's Eve celebration in Anono. The elaborate hierarchy of offices copied from the Catholic church was not implemented, however.

Unfortunately, the youth structure was not developed, and the young people were not encouraged to participate fully in the church. In fact, in many cases they were discouraged from doing so by the overwhelming conservative influence of their elders. Finding no responsible role to play in it, they left the church. It has been only within the past ten years that vigorous efforts have been being made to involve the young in the church.

The beginnings of the Harrist church can be divided into three periods. The first was characterized by the efforts of John Ahui and his assistants to spread Harris's message to people who had not previously heard it, as well as to encourage those people who were still trying to maintain their faith in spite of persecution by colonial authorities.

In a climate of growing nationalist ideology and the struggle for African autonomy, Ahui's efforts to actualize Harris's message brought forth the institutionalization of an indigenous Christian church of widespread appeal—created entirely on the basis of African initiative. This was the church's second developmental period.

The final phase, during the pre-Independence period of the 1950s, involved the expansion of the church to encompass all those who claimed to be Harrists. At this time, Ahui, as Harris's spiritual heir, became recognized as leader of all the Harrists; a standardized church structure and a doctrine began to be developed; and the Harrist Church of the Ivory Coast became a reality. All this occurred because of the brief ministry of one especially determined and charismatic African man.

CHAPTER 6

An Indigenous African Church

Traditional Structures
and Contemporary Organization

The development of the Harrist church was influenced by three factors: the indigenous village social structure, the directives of the Prophet Harris, and examples provided by the missionary churches.

The administrative organization of the church is composed of three levels: the elders, the apostles, and the ministers. Harris told the people he baptized to return to their villages and select twelve apostles and a minister to lead them in worship. The role of the elders as advisors is a continuation from the indigenous age-grade structure. A further category, the guardians, whose responsibility is to maintain order, is also a carry-over from the indigenous structure, in which the youngest age grade had a military function.

At present, each Harrist church ideally has three ministers who take turns officiating at services. In villages having many Harrists, there may be more than three ministers, and where there are few Harrists, there may be only one. A minister is chosen by the apostles, often from their ranks, and is approved by the congregation on the basis of criteria such as religious knowledge and fidelity, oratorical ability, upstanding character, and exemplary life-style. The man[1] chosen must be married, but monogamous,[2] must not drink alcohol to excess, and must be generally respected in the village. The ministers, including Ahui, receive no remuneration for their office, just as Harris accepted no payment for baptizing people. Like the members of their congregations, they work in Abidjan or are fishermen or craftsmen or small businessmen.

The ministers are held in high esteem by their congregations and often by non-Harrist villagers as well. Some church choirs create songs extolling the virtues of their ministers, thereby emphasizing their function in the community as role models. Amos-Djoro cites a song from M'Badon honoring the minister Peter Loba as a visible representative of the Holy Spirit on earth:

> The presence of Peter Loba
> Is not that of a man
> But rather that of God. [1956: 244]

A new minister may be installed by Ahui himself, or he may be both instructed in his duties and installed in office by the eldest minister in his village. Some new ministers go to Petit Bassam for instruction from Ahui. The training is not very extensive for a simple reason: the ministers are chosen precisely because they are believed to exhibit the proper qualities for the office already.

Actually, those people assumed to have the proper qualities to become ministers have tended to be selected according to criteria established by the traditional social structure. Age-grade status has remained a significant criterion. A minister has to be approved by his own age grade and by the eldest one. In the past it was essential for a minister to have been baptized by Harris. Now, however, most of those men are too old to be ministers and have become respected elders. Most ministers are from the second-oldest group, the group that furnishes the apostles, but some of these ministers have incurred opposition from church elders who consider them too young to occupy the position.

Such was the case for a minister in his middle forties who was appointed in 1965. Many villagers believed that he had the necessary qualities, and he wanted to be a minister. As he explained, however, "The old men said I was too young. They didn't want me to try to change things." Fortunately, the older brother of this man's father was the oldest man in the village and the senior elder in the church, and therefore had a great deal of influence in making the final decision. Without his uncle's help, the man believes that he never could have become a minister.

There is a tendency to expect that Harrist ministers will come from the same families, just as certain families furnished the priests of the traditional spirits in pre-Harris times. When Harris was in the Ivory Coast, in many cases the priests of the village spirits led their followers in adopting the new religious teachings. The Harrists are not unique in this tendency: the present Protestant minister of Abidjan-Santé is a member of the family that used to provide the priests of the village guardian spirit. At his death, Peter Loba, first Harrist minister of M'Badon, was succeeded by his son, also named Peter Loba. A younger brother of the present Peter Loba became, at the age of twenty-nine, the youngest Harrist apostle.

This is not to say that the office of minister has become institutionalized as hereditary. People consider it reasonable, however, for a son or younger brother to follow in the footsteps of his father or older brother, because he is judged to have the best opportunity to learn the knowledge and skills necessary for the office and he is aware of the respect and influence that the role of minister commands both in the village and in the wider Harrist community.

In Abobo-té, the nephew of Noé Tché-Tché, the first minister, also became a minister. Now this nephew's son hopes to pursue the same vocation. It is interesting that several of the educated young men who attended a conference of young Harrists in August 1972 were sons of Harrist ministers who expressed the desire to follow in the footsteps of their fathers. In a conversation one young man mentioned that his father was a minister; another said, "Oh. Then you will be a minister." This assumption is significant because members of this young educated group had in the past tended to leave the Harrist church for the higher-status Protestant and Catholic churches.

Within the ranks of the several hundred Harrist ministers, about thirty have been selected by Ahui for the special distinction of being "ministers with canes." These ministers carry cane-crosses like the bamboo one used by the Prophet Harris, a copy of which Harris presented to Ahui as a symbol of the mission that he was to undertake. The cane-crosses, identifying these men as continuing the mission of the prophet, are reminiscent of the gold staffs carried by representatives of the chiefs of the past.

Like the ministers empowered earlier by Ahui to aid him in spreading the new religion, the ministers with canes have the duty of traveling to different areas of the country to convert and baptize people into the Harrist church. They know more about Harrist doctrine and practice than other ministers and may be called upon to settle procedural disputes. To be a minister with a cane, a man must be recognized as being exceptionally dedicated to the Harrist church.

The major role of the Harrist ministers is to preach and to urge people to pray. The broader task of administering the church and of resolving the problems of the congregation belongs to the apostles. Although ideally numbering twelve, like the ministers they may number more or fewer than the ideal number, depending upon the size of the congregation. New apostles, selected by the ministers and other apostles, are approved by the congregation on the basis of their good character and their knowledge of village and church affairs, and also because of family ties.

The apostles are in charge of the temporal affairs of the church. They are responsible for the good conduct and obedience to church regulations of the members, including the ministers, whose behavior they also oversee. At their weekly meetings held at the home of the chief apostle, each apostle gives an accounting of his activities during the preceding week, which might include settling disputes between church members and resolving family quarrels. Collective solutions are sought to difficult problems. Just before the New Year begins, the apostles visit the homes of the church members to make sure that all quarrels will be settled before the old year ends, so that the New Year can start afresh. The intent is similar to that of the annual village purification ceremonies of the past.

The apostles also act as intermediaries between the congregation and the ministers. People who want to request blessings in church, or who want to confess and ask forgiveness for their misbehavior, explain their desires to the apostles. The apostles decide upon the validity of the members' requests and inform the ministers. During the church service an apostle, usually the chief apostle, states the supplicants' cases to the ministers and the congregation and publicly requests the officiating minister to bless them.

The apostles are also responsible for church finances, taking charge of spending collection money on church necessities and collecting larger sums from members to finance special projects such as big celebrations or the construction of a new church building. In the past, in order for a man to become an apostle, he had to be a member of the second-oldest age group. Now, however, there are younger apostles, as the youth of the church attempt to exercise a greater role in church affairs. When an apostle reaches the oldest age grade, he becomes an elder.

The elders serve as an advisory board to the apostles and to the ministers. Because some of them were alive when Harris came to the Ivory Coast, and in many cases were baptized by him (or a disciple), they are repositories of information about what may or may not be done in keeping with his dictates. The elders have the power of vetoing selections for the offices of minister or apostle and of approving or overruling proposed changes in church practice.

Another important role in the church is that of the guardians, or "guards of God." They keep order during church services and enforce the punishment meted out to transgressors of church rules by the apostles. During services the guardians stand at the altar rail with switches that they rap on the rail when members of the congregation talk or disturb others. They also walk around the church tapping with their switches people who continue talking or who fall asleep. Children are treated tolerantly and are allowed to move freely around during the church services unless they begin to disturb people. Most guardians are young to middle-aged men, but sometimes young boys also learn to keep order in the church.

In addition to these four major male role statuses in the church organization, most other church members also have a specific role to play. The role structure of the church is visible in the seating pattern during services. Women sit on the left and men on the right of the center aisle, an arrangement the Harrists share with the Catholic and Protestant churches.

The front rows of both sides are occupied by the choir of young men and women that leads the congregation in song. Most songs are sung to the rhythm of beaded gourd rattles, and a few wealthy churches also have organs. Members of the choir compose and set to music their own songs, which consequently vary from village to village. Although villagers learn new songs from each other, occasionally in the languages of different ethnic groups, most songs are sung in the language of the congregation. A few songs are composed in French.

Behind the choir on both sides sit the children and the young people who are not part of the choir. Behind them on the women's side are the women responsible for laundering the ministers' robes and the sweepers who help to keep the church and church grounds clean. The elderly women, who because of their venerable age no longer perform such tasks, occupy the rows in the rear. Behind the young people on the men's side sit the men responsible for ringing the bell to summon the congregation to services. Behind them sit the men who light the candles that decorate the altar, and behind them the sweepers who share with their female counterparts the responsibility for keeping the church and grounds clean. Off-duty guardians sit at the rear.

Although not everyone has a specifically assigned duty, there are enough roles so that most members of the congregation can have a sense of personal responsibility in the functioning of the church. There is no automatic progression from one role to another in a definite hierarchy, and a person may occupy the same function for most of his or her life. This sense of order and group involvement is important to the Harrists, who cite it as one factor that makes them unique among the Christian churches.

In some villages there is a committee that crosscuts the different statuses in the church. This committee, comprised of representatives from the ministers, apostles, guardians, and choir, meets to discuss church policy and plan activities such as celebrations and visits to other villages. The committee discusses issues such as the responsibilities of the church in the village and nation, and how well it is fulfilling them, as well as appropriate methods to increase attendance and membership. The committee also presents condolences to the bereaved, helps to settle disputes, and disseminates information among the various groups in the church.

In 1961 a national central committee comprised of delegates from various Harrist churches was created. The existence of Le Comité de la Mission Harriste en Côte d'Ivoire was officialized with an announcement in the *Journal Officiel de la République de la Côte d'Ivoire*:

Declaration of Association

According to Decree No. 3050 I. CAB. AG. of the Ministry of the Interior of the Republic of the Ivory Coast, there has been created an association by the name of "Church of Christ Harrist Mission" of which the headquarters is in Petit Bassam, at the home of Monsieur John Ahui, P.O. 3356, Adjamé, and having as a goal: to unite all of the persons who declare themselves to be of the Harrist religion and to be subject to the authority of the supreme prophet "John Ahui," P.O. 3356, Adjamé. [*Journal Officiel de la République de la Côte d'Ivoire*, 4 March 1961: 328]

The committee set for itself these tasks: to create a national organization representing all Harrists; to determine by which criteria religious groups claiming to be in the tradition of the prophet would be accepted as Harrists; and to create a sense of allegiance among members of all these groups to the Harrist Church of the Ivory Coast led by John Ahui.[3]

It is endeavoring to create a standard doctrine and set of procedures to be followed by all Harrists. This group also represents the Harrists to official bodies such as the Ivorian government. A major task of the central committee has been to try to gather the resources to create in Abidjan a headquarters for the Harrist mission, to include a large church, a guest house, and teaching and recreational facilities for young people. This committee is also concerned with creating a favorable image for the Harrist church in the nation, as well as with trying to spread the church to areas not yet evangelized.

The Temples of the Prophet

A Harrist church building, particularly if it is relatively new, is usually the most outstanding edifice in the village. The architecture and decor of those churches where funds permit are elaborate and unique. The building of a church is a major event in the lives of the members. They contribute monthly to a building fund that may continue for years. A number of villages have unfinished buildings, larger and more elaborate than the existing structures, on which they work as finances permit. In M'Badon, for example, a new one-thousand-seat building, which when finished will be the largest Harrist church, was begun several years ago. In Abobo-Doumé the first stone of a new church was laid in 1957, but the building was not finished until 1969 because of the difficulty of raising money for materials.

The simple style of the older (1950s) cement structures resembles that of Protestant churches, a similarity that requires no special explanation. The unusual, eye-catching design of many newer buildings calls for comment, however. Many Harrist churches, handsome white buildings with two towers, somewhat resemble Muslim mosques because of the influence of Islamic brickmasons who helped to build them. The Islamic architectural style inspired an original model that allows the Harrists to distinguish their structures from those of the Protestants and the Catholics.

Some of the older Harrist churches are very austere both inside and outside. Others are adorned with murals and other decorative features, and some have photographs on the walls of the Prophet Harris, John Ahui in Liberia with the prophet, and a variety of religious scenes. Exteriors and interiors of Harrist churches are painted white. The support columns of many of the churches are painted in the national colors: orange, white, and green. The church in Abobo-Doumé has small stained-glass windows also in the national colors. All churches have simple wooden pews aligned facing the pulpit on either side of the aisle. The raised pulpit area includes high-backed chairs for the ministers and a lectern with a Bible on it from which they preach. There are pews for the apostles on one side of the ministers' chairs and for the elders on the other.

The most austere churches have only a large wooden cross before a wooden altar and reflect a strict adherence to the prophet's edict against worshiping representations of spiritual beings. Other churches have a statue of Harris near the altar, and one occasionally finds statues of angels in Harrist churches. In the church in Petit Bassam there is a statue of Harris at either side of the altar. One of the statues represents the prophet himself, and the other, John Ahui, who, like other Harrist ministers, dresses exactly as Harris did. In the Petit Bassam church there are two statues of angels that were a gift, and statues of angels also constitute part of the exterior decor of the church in Abidjan-Santé.

These statues of angels, of obvious Catholic influence, have come to represent a problem to the Harrists, because according to Harrist doctrine, no one has ever seen God or any other spiritual being, and therefore one should not try to represent them. Harris commanded his followers to hate idolatry, yet these representations of spiritual beings show a marked similarity, perceptible to many Harrists, to the ritual objects Harris told his converts to destroy.

The church in Abobo-té at one time contained statues of Harris, of angels, and also of Saint Michael slaying a dragon. The elders, however, realized that the statues were incompatible with Harrist doctrine and had them removed. Only the statue of Harris remains, in a booth at the entrance to the chief minister's courtyard, across the street from the church. Harrists agree that their churches should have a statue of the prophet, to honor the man who brought Christianity to the Ivory Coast.

The church in Abobo-Doumé is quite ornate. At the altar, in addition to the statue of Harris, there is a crucifix; although it is not the only crucifix found in a Harrist church, it contrasts with the empty cross more appropriate to the Harrist churches. The crucifix is a symbolic remnant of Catholicism rather than an element of significance for the Harrists. The cross is a central symbol because Harris carried one and because it is believed that in the cross resides great spiritual power capable of combating the forces of evil, not because Jesus Christ was crucified.

The great importance of the cross to the Harrists is evident in the midnight ceremony in which the cross is placed before the altar to consecrate a church. Ahui and the ministers, apostles, and elders of the church are present, and the church officials confess their sins to Ahui. The placing of the cross may be seen as a kind of purification of the church and its leaders, similar to a re-creation of Harris's initial baptism with his cross. The Harrist minister who described this ceremony said, "The cross releases a powerful force, and when a person walks into a Harrist church and sees the cross, together with the Bible on the pulpit, the person feels a great spiritual force." Thus, the cross has retained the kind of meaning that the prophet's cross had for his converts, as a seat of power that works to dispel evil.

On the wall behind the altar in the Abobo-Doumé church is a colorful triptych. The three panels depict, respectively, a hand, presumably from heaven, giving a golden key to a bearded, haloed man standing before an array of impressive-looking modern buildings; a white-haired elderly white man in an African setting, as represented by a variety of animals, with the sun on one side of his head and the moon on the other, and a lightning bolt behind his upraised hand; and Saint Michael slaying a dragon.

The first panel represents humankind receiving the key to what might be interpreted to mean material prosperity in the present life.

The second indicates the arrival of Christianity in the Ivory Coast, and therefore the origin of the Harrist church, because Harris brought the Christian god to the Ivorians. The portrayal of God as white is said by Harrist leaders to be unimportant because God is spirit and therefore neither white nor black. Actually, of course, he should not be portrayed at all, because no one has seen him.

The panel of Saint Michael slaying the dragon represents human-kind's conquest over evil, the Harrists' ultimate goal. This is an image that is found in other Harrist churches in either paint or statuary form. Saint Michael, who is believed to have slain evil spirits, symbolizes the power of Christianity in the supreme battle between good and evil. The triptych thus portrays the idea that, when Harris brought knowledge of the Christian god to the Ivory Coast, he also gave the Ivorians arms with which to fight against evil, helping them to attain salvation as represented by a prosperous life in contemporary society.

The Life of the Church

KEEPING THE FAITH

Harrist church services are held seven times per week. There are three services on Sunday, at 5:00 A.M., 9:00 A.M., and 3:30 P.M. Tuesday and Thursday services are held at 7:00 P.M., and there are early morning services on Wednesday and Friday at 5:00 A.M. In some villages, the early morning and evening services last only a half hour instead of the usual hour. The Sunday 9:00 A.M. service is the best attended, whereas attendance at the early morning services, where there are prayers, songs, and blessings, but no sermon, is less.

The bestowing of blessings is an important aspect of Harrist worship. People ask for blessings before important undertakings, such as major fishing, agricultural, or business ventures, and before big celebrations. They may also confess real or potential transgressions and receive blessings to absolve them of blame and subsequent misfortune. Blessings may also be requested in cases of illness. During the part of the service when the blessings are bestowed, people give thanks to God for their success or good fortune, for having escaped unharmed from an accident, or for having recovered from an illness. They pray to have children and thank God when children are born.

People who desire blessings, having first received the approval of the apostles and the consent of the ministers, come forward at the designated time in the service and kneel on the steps before the altar. The individual or the leader of the group explains the reason for the blessing to the chief apostle, who repeats it for the ministers and the congregation, making comments as he deems appropriate. The ministers come from behind the altar and stand in front of the supplicants. The presiding minister touches the head of each individual with the Bible and then, with his eyes closed and the Bible open in his hands, says a prayer. The members of the congregation bow their heads in reverence, and the other ministers stand with their hands palms up in a prayerful gesture. After the prayer, the ministers shake the hands of the people blessed, who then return to their places. Sometimes the choir begins a song to ask God to bless the supplicants.

It is customary to request a blessing after there has been a death in the family. During a Sunday service observed in Abobo-Doumé, a group of about twenty people led by a prominent and respected apostle requested a blessing. A member of the family had died, and the survivors wished to purify themselves for any transgressions that they might have committed during the funeral: in their grief, they might have thought or spoken unkindly of others with no real intention of doing evil.

Ministers, too, may request blessings from their colleagues. On another occasion in Abobo-Doumé one of the ministers asked for a blessing, proceeding in the same fashion as did other members of the congregation. The church was planning a celebration and he asked God that it go well. The subsequent Sunday he went through the same procedure, this time to give thanks to God for his help in the success of the celebration.

Non-Harrists may also request blessings in the Harrist church. They may accompany Harrist relatives for a blessing after a death in the family or may, as individuals, ask for blessings after committing acts defined as sins by the Harrists, but not by their own church.

Harrists explain that, because of the relative newness of the church, the frequent services are necessary in order to attract more members, as well as to intensify the involvement of present members. Some Harrists speak positively of these frequent services because they keep members constantly aware of the need to be good Christians, in stark contrast to churches that have services only on Sundays and are closed for the rest of the week. Harrists say that many of these "Sunday Christians" have a tendency to seek other kinds of spiritual support during the week—the kinds of indigenous spiritual support prohibited by the prophet and made unnecessary by the Harrist church. By providing frequent spiritual communion for its members, the Harrist church keeps its members aware of its sufficiency to meet all of their spiritual needs.

The Harrists are not unique in having such frequent services. In some villages the Protestants also have numerous weekly services for the same reasons—to allow their members to feel that they are continually protected by God and to intensify their sense of exclusive reliance on the church. The Harrists say that the Protestants imitated them in this matter. Although many Harrists feel secure in being able to attend church so often, some young people in particular are not enthusiastic about the expectation of such frequent attendance.

Everyone must wear white to church. Ministers wear long white robes with black bands crossing their chests and little round white hats, imitating Harris's attire. The elders wear draped togas, and the other men wear white slacks or shorts and shirts. Women wear long wrapped white cloths, blouses, and head wraps. Harrists wear white both in imitation of Harris and as an expression of the state of purity from sin in which they present themselves before their god. They question the state of purity in which members of other churches, who do not wear white to church, present themselves before their god.

MAKING A JOYFUL NOISE
UNTO THE LORD

The services follow a definite pattern, of which the Sunday 9:00 A.M. service provides the most complete example. The bell ringer rings the bell first at 8:30 to remind people that they should be nearly ready to leave for church, and a second time at 8:45 to summon the congregation to gather at the home of the chief minister, where he blesses them with a prayer such as "Our Father, protect us from the evil spirits at this time as we go into the temple." Then, led by the three ministers, the congregation begins its procession to the church, singing with no instrumental accompaniment. The crowd grows in size and enthusiasm as members who missed the benediction join the procession. Arriving at the church, the congregation enters solemnly and members take their places. Some people, including the ministers, remove their shoes before entering the church as a sign of respect. Others, presumably those of Catholic background, genuflect and make the sign of the cross upon entering the church. Some kneel briefly in the aisle and pray before taking a seat. People who arrive late during a prayer wait respectfully outside until a song begins.

The order of a typical Sunday morning service is as follows, as exemplified by the church in Abobo-Doumé:

Processional song

Prayer by the minister
Lord's Prayer in unison by the congregation
Song
Prayer by the minister
Lord's Prayer in unison by the congregation
Song
Blessings of the people who had requested them
Sermon
Song interrupting the sermon
Continuation of the sermon
Church information and announcements
Recessional song (sung outside after congregation leaves the church)

The contents of the components of this service were:

Processional song:

At the sound of the bell
We go to the Holy Church
To confess to the All Powerful God
Our sins in order to be pardoned.
Before the arrival of the Prophet William Wade Harris
We were just vulgar fetishers.

The practice of fetishism is
Forbidden to us by our Prophet.
Whoever would like to continue worshiping fetishes
Will lead himself to hell.

Prayer by the minister:

Oh God, Our Father, we ask your blessing for all of the faithful
who believe in your salvation.

We ask you also to lessen the pain of all those who are presently
ill in body and spirit.

We ask you to give us the strength necessary to continue the
work of the Prophet William Wade Harris in order to save all of
humanity from the evil that surrounds it.

[Harrist prayers often ask blessings for the whole village and
the entire population of the Ivory Coast, including specifically
the members of the government and the president of the
republic.]

Song:

On this earth we recognize
That we are eternal sinners.
We implore Our God, therefore,
To accord us his pardon for our sins.

Prayer by the minister:

Oh, Our God, we pray for the Prophet John Ahui in order that
he may have the strength to persevere always in the task confided
in him by the Prophet William Wade Harris, your messenger.

Oh, God, You alone can give him this strength that will permit
him to accomplish this task well.

Song:

As Christ said, dear faithful believers,
We must follow our hearts and truly pray to God.
If we do not have faith,
It is sincerely useless to come to church
At each ringing of the bell
To satisfy the eyes of others,
Whereas in ourselves the devil lives.

Because of what does the meaning of our faith consist
If as soon as we come out of church
We already think of evil?

Sermon:

[The theme was that all believers in and followers of the
Prophet Harris must be inspired by a desire to help the weak and
give to the poor to the extent of the giver's possibilities.]

Song interrupting the sermon:

We are on earth
And we say the name of God for nothing
[without giving it the proper importance].
We must associate our hearts
To the invocation of the name of God.
And believe in Him and follow Him.

Continuation of the sermon:

A rich follower of Jesus Christ asked him one day, "Oh Lord,
what can I do to enter heaven?" Christ answered him in these
words, "Faith is a sacrifice, and to enter heaven, you must
sacrifice a bit of yourself. For your prayers to be answered you
must do only this: distribute to the poor that of which you have
more than they, and the door of heaven will be open to you."

Church information and announcements:

[The major announcement concerned the upcoming anniversary celebration of the completion of the church building in
Abobo-Doumé. The tenor of the announcement was in keeping
with the theme of the sermon. For the occasion, all of the women
in the church planned to make new garments of the same fabric.
Those women who had sufficient money to pay for the material
were urged to contribute extra money so that those women with
insufficient funds would also be able to have garments. The
minister said that if only three women in the congregation had
money, all of the women should be able to have garments.]

Recessional song:

After reflecting, we are led to recognize

That we had always endured a certain suffering.
During this period, the Prophet William Wade Harris had not yet appeared.
But when he did come to us to bring us the Sacred News,
And the blessing of the All Powerful,
He did not receive the most enthusiastic welcome possible
Because we did not know that he was the bringer of the message that would liberate us.
Now we realize that he was one of the messengers of God.
Dear brothers and sisters
We send out to you a call to the faith forever.

The congregation also exits according to the order of seating and assembles in front of the church. The choir starts a song with which the people join in by singing and dancing. When the ministers reach the awaiting congregation, they lead the group in a lively procession down the main street of the village. The gourd rattles provide rhythm for the recessional songs, to which church members, especially women, dance animatedly down the street.

Non-Harrists gather along the sides of the street to watch. When the procession passes the Protestant church, the singing and dancing stop so as to not disturb the service, and resume beyond the church. Several times during the procession the ministers stop and a group of women dances around them. Occasionally, the most dynamic of the ministers joins the women and dances enthusiastically around the other ministers. The joyous procession continues to the home of the eldest minister. There, after a final lively encore of dancing, the congregation kneels and the minister pronounces a final benediction. Having celebrated their god and having protected themselves against evil, everyone then returns home.

THE BIBLE AND VILLAGE LIFE

Sermons consist of moral exhortations based on biblical themes. The minister or a young person may read biblical passages in French and then translate them into the vernacular. The Harrists, like members of other religions, select those passages from the Bible that coincide with their own particular world view. Subjects of sermons include such topics as the prohibition of adultery, the necessity of respecting authority, the importance of observing the Sabbath, the necessity of being kind to friends and neighbors, and the danger of worshiping false gods. The minister in Abobo-Doumé cited a biblical passage about worshiping false gods, for example, in a sermon on the evils of the traditional religion and the wonders of the Christian god. This minister holds Bible classes for young people at his home, where they read and interpret passages from the Scriptures and sing songs.

The Lord's Prayer is recited by the congregation two or three times during a service—after each of the minister's prayers. This was the first Christian prayer that many people baptized by Harris were taught, which perhaps accounts for its significance. Bianquis found that some of the people who had been baptized by Harris, and continued to pray to God with their fellow villagers, knew nothing of Christian prayer except the Lord's Prayer—sometimes in English, which they did not understand (1924: 1145). Perhaps the Lord's Prayer acquired special significance because it was initially the only way Harris's converts knew of communicating with his god.

ENTERING HIS PRESENCE WITH SINGING

The songs sung by the Harrists have great social as well as religious significance. At the 1972 Congress of Young Harrist Intellectuals, there was discussion about streamlining church services, yet the suggestion that fewer songs be sung was vehemently rejected. The songs have moral content; that is, they are believed to exert a special influence on the singer and listener. Their message affects people's hearts and consciences, making them aware of any evil thoughts they may have and thus helping them to eliminate such thoughts. Songs praise the Prophet Harris for bringing the Ivorians out of their previous spiritual darkness, ask pardon for sins, exhort people to behave correctly, and the like. Many are based upon ideas drawn from the Bible, often corresponding to themes addressed in sermons. When these themes are mentioned, the choir may spontaneously break into song, interrupting the minister. When he feels that enough stanzas have been sung, he rings a bell to signal the choir to stop. The choir may, however, with good-humored defiance, continue singing along enthusiastically.

Processions are an integral part of all seven weekly Harrist services. One explanation given for their importance is that "God is life. God is joy. Joy doesn't kill. So the Harrists worship God joyfully." Harris, when asked by a missionary the purpose of the gourd rattle he carried to provide rhythmic accompaniment to his songs, is said to have responded that God wanted people to praise him with music and that the rattles made sufficient noise for him to hear the people's songs. The Harrist processions are thus a manifestation of the joyousness of their style of worship, as well as a continuation of a form of festive celebration traditional to the lagoons people.

The Harrist procession may also be seen as a re-creation of the events of Harris's reception by the villagers to whom he preached. He and his followers would enter a village singing to the accompaniment of the gourd rattles. Hearing them, the villagers would go to welcome them and to escort them to the center of the village, where they would listen to the prophet's message. In keeping with local custom, and as a gesture of respect, after he shared his message with them, they would escort him to where he was staying. The habit of assembling at the home of the chief minister to walk with the ministers to church, and then accompanying the chief minister back to his compound, may be interpreted as a reenactment of the reception given to Harris (when he was properly received, of course). Thus, the original procession became institutionalized as part of the church ritual.

Processions are also a major feature of the Harrists' eclectic observation of religious holidays. In addition to Christmas and Easter, they also celebrate Ascension and the Feast of Pentecost. The latter are national holidays, as a result of the French Catholic colonial influence, but hold no special significance in the context of Harrist doctrine. The All Saints' Day celebration held in the Harrist village of Bregbo draws crowds of Harrists and spectators from as far away as Ghana. On this occasion, the Harrists have an elaborate procession, singing and dancing gaily up and down the main street of the village to the syncopated rhythm of rattles and drums. This renowned celebration has been featured several times on national television.

Crowds of spectators, as well as Harrists from surrounding and distant villages, travel each year to the village of Anono to attend the New Year's celebration. Beginning at midnight and continuing for hours, the Harrists parade up and down the main street singing and dancing, carrying lit candles. This celebration is similar to the village purification ceremonies of pre-Harris days, in which flaming branches were used to chase away evil spirits. Those celebrations were also held in preparation for the coming of the New Year.

The most important annual Harrist celebration is the Rain Feast, held on 27 July at Petit Bassam. Falling at the end of the long rainy season, it is essentially a harvest feast replacing the traditional Yam Feast that once was the major yearly celebration. Several Harrist villages and a number of government officials are invited to participate in the festivities and feasting. The minister thanks God for the harvest and explains the biblical meaning attributed to the celebration. The long rainy season recalls to the Harrists the time when, according to the Bible, the earth was destroyed by the flood. They give thanks to God that this will not occur again. Members of the participating churches make special uniforms for the occasion and spend the day socializing and dancing. There is also a procession especially for the visiting ministers from other villages. This celebration, too, is sometimes televised.

Other occasions observed by all Harrists are the Feast of John Ahui on 3 December, celebrating the day he returned from Liberia, and the Feast of the Prophet Harris on 14 June, commemorating the deliverance of the Harrists from darkness by their prophet. Many villages also have celebrations of their own to commemorate special occasions or events, such as the Festival of the Children in M'Badon, which expresses the villagers' thanks to God that the number of children born in the village increased dramatically once they received the Prophet Harris's message. Some villages have feasts on the anniversary of the completion of their new church building. Thus the Harrist church is an expressive joyful religion in which divine blessings are celebrated with song and dance.

Thou Shalt Not . . .

Gaiety is only one facet of the Harrist religion. Harrist doctrine also, like other religions, includes a number of prohibitions, the violation of which constitutes more or less serious sins, and all of which are believed to have been proscribed by the Prophet Harris. Harris strictly forbade lying, theft, alcoholism, adultery, and working on the Sabbath. Lying, theft, and adultery were already considered reprehensible acts according to indigenous morality. Furthermore, people did not work on the days dedicated to their protective spirits; so some of the prophet's admonitions corresponded to and reinforced indigenous mores. Harris's prohibition of excessive drinking was a result of his Protestant training, as well as of his desire to encourage the Ivorians to work diligently for their own social and economic progress.

The prophet was particularly adamant about the observance of the Sabbath. Some younger Harrists believe that the institutionalization in the church of this prohibition also had pragmatic intentions and results. The founders of the Harrist church wanted the new Christians to become thoroughly imbued with this religion and wanted them to have no activities that might distract them from attending church on Sunday and spending the day worshiping God. The prohibition continues in effect today, and most Harrists do spend a good portion of the day attending church, resting, and sometimes attending Harrist gatherings at which they sing and dance.

One Harrist offered two tales about people who had been punished for not respecting the Sabbath. One man who went to hunt on a Sunday came upon a deer and drew his gun to shoot. Suddenly the deer spoke to him, saying that he was not supposed to be working on Sunday and that everyone, including the animals, should spend the day resting and praying to the Christian god. Undaunted, the man tried to shoot the deer again and again. Having failed in his attempts, he returned home, told the story of the talking deer, and fell dead.

Another man is said to have gone with his son to chop down a tree on a Sunday. When the tree was almost cut through and ready to fall, it re-formed itself. The man tried to chop it down a second time and it regenerated itself. On his third attempt, he turned into a tree. His son returned home to tell the story. Respect for the Sabbath, then, is taken very seriously. One young man reported that when he was in secondary school his father did not even want him to study on Sunday.

A sin considered very serious by the Harrists, and said to have been specifically prohibited by the prophet, is having sexual relations out-of-doors, actually a traditional prohibition that already existed among the lagoons ethnic groups. Like many other West African peoples, they considered having sexual relations on the ground to be an offense against the ancestors buried in the earth. The ancestors might respond to the offense by causing misfortune to the guilty parties, or to the entire village. The guilty parties would then have to confess and make sacrifices to propitiate the angry ancestors. Harrists now explain this prohibition by saying that it is what animals do and that people who sin in this way are acting like animals and offending the Christian god, who wants humans to act in a more dignified manner. This important traditional prohibition has thus been given a new interpretation by being attributed to Harris.

The most serious of all sins is that of "eating human flesh and drinking human blood"—committing witchcraft. The commandments "Thou shalt not eat human flesh; thou shalt not drink human blood" are carved, along with other less ominous-sounding ones, on the facades of some Harrist churches. This language is, of course, purely symbolic. The cannibalism referred to is totally abstract and strictly "at a distance." The act of wishing someone ill is regarded as efficacious. A person known or discovered to have had a bad relationship with another person who is sick or who dies will be suspected of having caused the illness or death by eating the person's flesh and drinking the person's blood, abstractly, "from a distance," "as a devil."

To practice witchcraft is the ultimate sin in the Harrist church because of the devastating effects witchcraft has on social relationships and on the functioning of the society. Because of the fear and social malaise it causes, its prevention and punishment are major Harrist preoccupations. The practice of witchcraft or fear or threat thereof can prevent people from enjoying the fruits of their labors or inhibit their efforts and ambitions.

A person who is revealed to have commited the ultimate sin of witchcraft must first confess to the council of apostles, who request that the minister ask God to pardon the guilty individual. The person must then make a full public confession in church so that the entire congregation is aware of the deed. Then the ministers, the apostles, and the congregation must pray to God to forgive the person. In effect, therefore, the person who commits a sin against the social order must first ask to be forgiven by the members of the community before God's forgiveness can be asked.

Looking toward the Future

The 1955 Harrist conference called for greater participation of young people in the church. Their increased involvement has been a gradual process because the gerontocratic, age-graded organizational structure provides for increased involvement and influence only with increasing age.[4] Starting in the 1960s, however, youth committees have been being created in some villages, at meetings of which young Harrists gather to discuss their possible contribution to the church. An embryonic national youth committee, the Union de la Jeunesse Harriste de Côte d'Ivoire, has been in existence since 1966.

The most significant activity undertaken by this group has been the organization of a conference held on 24–26 August 1972 in M'Badon.[5] The first Congress of Young Harrist Intellectuals[6] was chaired by Dr. Bruno Claver, who as a student had edited the *Premier livret de l'education religieuse à l'usage des missions Harristes*. Now a highly educated neuropsychiatrist, Claver has resumed his leadership role in the church, giving special encouragement to efforts to modernize and standardize church practices. Albert Atcho, president of the national committee and a famous traditional healer,[7] was the congress's honorary president.

The conference was attended by about one hundred people, mostly between the ages of twenty and twenty-five years. With only two exceptions, all were male. There were a few older church leaders present, who clarified for the young people some of the principles behind elements of church practice.

Claver briefly discussed Harris's activities and his effect on the Ivory Coast, noting that 1973 would mark the sixtieth anniversary of the year in which "the son of Africa, William Wade Harris, came and tore away the veil of shadows." He emphasized how great the Liberian prophet's influence had been, to have had such a broad and lasting effect, when he had had time to teach only the most rudimentary elements of Christianity and no time at all to set up an organization to perpetuate his teachings. Furthermore, the continuance of his teaching had been entrusted to men who had had no formal training and who were subject to persecution by the colonial administration for their religious activities. The movement had nonetheless persevered, although because of the myriad of obstacles put in its path, it was not until the 1950s that it had begun to prosper.

In this context one participant mentioned that many members of the Harrist church were uninformed or misinformed about the life of the Prophet Harris and the history of the development of the church, and that different people held different opinions about the same events. Others expressed annoyance about the incorrect information that had been written about the church and its history by non-Harrists. Claver assured them that members of the church had been working for some time on a history of the church expressly for the purposes of teaching Harrists about their own history and providing an accurate account for outsiders.

Many people, Claver continued, had characterized the Harrist church as a "religion of old men" that would disappear when they died. He urged the young people present to begin immediately to shoulder the important task of assuming responsibility for assuring its future. This conference marked the first step in the process. It provided the first opportunity for young people as a group to have formal input into church decision making. That the conference had the approval of the national committee indicated the church leaders' sincerity about increasing the involvement of the young.

The young people's task was to discuss the structure and functioning of the church, and to suggest changes that, from their perspective, seemed desirable. Under Claver's guidance, documents had been prepared in advance of the meeting to provide a basis for discussion. After these documents were read aloud during the initial plenary session, the delegates separated into workshops to discuss the issues raised. Workshop participants' responses and suggestions were summarized and discussed in a final plenary session.

An extensive discussion concerning the training and behavior of Harrist ministers took place. The young people were distressed at what they saw as the poor quality of some ministers. They regarded this problem as most fundamental, because the behavior of these leaders could cause Harrists to leave the church and outsiders to scorn it. They insisted that ministers should set positive behavioral examples for their congregations, particularly with respect to such issues as alcohol consumption and monogamy.

The young people felt very strongly that their ministers needed to be better educated and more knowledgeable about church history and doctrine. They urged that henceforth all ministers should be literate, so that they might read the Bible and explain it to their congregations, and were pleased to learn of plans to establish a seminary in M'Badon to train Harrist ministers.

Participants expressed concern at the diversity that continues to exist between churches, largely because of the rapid expansion of the movement and the differences in the ministers' preparation and knowledge. Some literate ministers, for example, make considerable use of the Bible, whereas others do not. Also, different ministers have varying ideas about what constitutes church history, policy, and doctrine. One participant described an incident that took place during a church service. An older minister and a younger one argued about whether Harris had stopped in their village and whether the cane-cross that Harris carried and the cross in the church contained spirits or were just empty pieces of wood. The young men felt that such an occurrence was regrettable, but also exemplary of the need to compile an accurate church history and to teach a standardized doctrine to all ministers.

In some localities, elements of local custom are considered to be a part of formal Harrist doctrine, a situation the young delegates thought could be rectified by the uniform training of ministers. It was also suggested that new ministers should spend time as apprentices in villages of different ethnic groups, to get to know them, so as to be better able to serve the interests of Harrist unity.

Another enthusiastically discussed issue concerned modifying church services. There was some discussion about whether there should be fewer services, but it was concluded that the elders would not approve such a suggestion and that the number of services was not excessive, provided that they lasted no more than the allotted hour or half-hour. It was recommended that henceforth services in all villages follow the same schedule and include reading and commentary on biblical texts as well as reflections on problems of everyday life. The suggestion was also made that the theme of each Sunday's service be uniform in all churches so that all Harrists would meditate on the same ideas at the same time.

For many of the young people the conference was the first opportunity to seek clarification of the reasons behind certain church practices. On the basis of their greater understanding, they could begin to examine which features were fundamental and which had lost or might lose their meaning under changed circumstances. One important item discussed, for example, was respect of the Sabbath. Because some Harrists now hold jobs in the modern sector requiring working on Sunday, the issue has acquired nuances that it did not have when the population engaged largely in fishing and agriculture. Some people thought that the basic principle was that one should not seek financial gain on the Sabbath, but this, an elder informed them, was not the fundamental issue. After thorough discussion of various aspects of the issue, the participants arrived at the understanding that, although there were duties that might require performance of some type of work on the Sabbath, one should do one's best to dedicate Sundays to religious activities.

Participants expressed the desire for the church as an institution to become a more significant force in the secular lives of its members. For example, it was stated that Harrist parents were not sufficiently responsible in assuring that their children went to school and did their homework. To remedy this problem, it was suggested that the village committees should assume the responsibility of monitoring the education of Harrist children. In this vein participants reaffirmed the importance of working toward the creation of the youth organization, "The Pioneers of the Prophet," that had originally been proposed at the 1955 conference. Its purpose would be to provide educational, recreational, and service activities for children and adolescents. Conferees also talked about ways to raise money for educational and other church service projects. One man suggested that church members establish fishing, farming, and transportation cooperatives to raise money for these projects. The social significance of these issues implies that the young people attending this conference thought that the Harrist church should work more to promote communitarian interests and assume greater collective responsibility for the secular as well as the spiritual welfare of its members.

Throughout the conference there was an emphasis on affirming the uniqueness of the Harrist church and on eliminating external influences from it. For example, church construction and decor were discussed in this context. Some participants thought that both decor and building style should be standardized to conform to a typically Harrist style. They especially regretted that some of their churches were indistinguishable from Protestant structures. The other fundamental issue discussed concerned the creation of uniform standards within the church institution. A reigning idea of the conference was that a Harrist should be able to go to a Harrist church in any village of any ethnic group and at once find himself or herself in familiar surroundings.

The conference was a grand success. The participants departed with a spirit of enthusiasm about what they had learned. They had developed many interesting suggestions for changes, some more feasible than others, and their suggestions were to be shared with the village and national committees for consideration. The young men anticipated resistance from their elders regarding many of their suggestions, because the elders usually insisted that the church was as the Prophet Harris had dictated, and so must remain unchanged. Predictably, older men present at the conference had responded to some of the proposed changes with the argument, "The Prophet Harris did not say that."

The Congress of Young Harrist Intellectuals represented an attempt to continue the process begun in the 1955 conference, but with a greater sense of urgency. Having taken the stand that Harrism is not just "a religion of old men," the Harrists are now trying to live up to their aspirations. The leaders acknowledge the necessity of adapting aspects of church practice to a changing life-style, and they recognize the crucial role of the young in this process. The young people are requesting more answers and explanations and are offering more suggestions. They want to take active roles in modifying the church in keeping with the political and economic realities of contemporary Ivorian life.

CHAPTER 7

The Religion of the Africans

The Ebrié Influence

Because the Prophet Harris spent the longest and most effective period of his career in Ebrié territory, most of the Harrists are Ebrié. Another reason for the large representation of Ebrié among the Harrists is that the members of the delegation who went to see Harris in Liberia were all Ebrié, as were the ministers who assisted John Ahui in continuing the prophet's mission, and they proselytized among the people who were most accessible to them.[1]

Of the fifty-six Ebrié villages, there are not more than three that do not have a group of Harrists of some size and a Harrist church of some description, from a simple tin-roofed structure to an elaborate concrete building. The village of M'Badon is 100 percent Harrist. Anono is divided about equally between Harrists and Catholics; Petit Bassam is divided between Harrists and Protestants; and of the approximately one thousand villagers of Abobo-Doumé, slightly more than two-fifths are Harrists, slightly less than two-fifths are Catholics, and about one-fifth are Protestants.

The Alladian and Attié, the next most numerous ethnic groups in the church, are the closest neighbors of the Ebrié, and the Ebrié recognize ties of kinship with both groups. Harris did not travel inland to Attié country, and he spent very little time among the Alladian; so the relatively large proportion of Harrists from these two groups is attributable to the influence of the clerk-disciples who perpetuated Harris's work in those areas, as well as to the efforts of Ahui and his assistants to bring them into the church.

The Ebrié live in the coastal region where Abidjan, the nation's capital, is located. This is the most technologically developed area of the country and has the highest standard of living. Much of Ebrié

117

land is now dedicated to coffee, cocoa, and oil palm plantations that are worked mostly by laborers from less affluent African countries. R. Bouscayrol reported that there were attractive cement houses in Ebrié villages before 1938, owned by villagers who had become wealthy during a period when cocoa and coffee were selling for very good prices. Concerning the effects of this new affluence and the consequences of Ebrié proximity to the growing capital, he wrote:

> This evolution is taking place, however, without violent shocks and in a way marginal to that of the cosmopolitan elements of the [newly] implanted capital. The Ebrié still prefers the calm of his village to the urban activity, and when a young man works in the city, he returns in the evening to the family homestead where one sleeps far from the chants of Islam and safe from the nocturnal thieves. [Bouscayrol 1949: 384, 404]

Although this was written in 1949, a similar situation holds true today, and the Harrist church remains a village phenomenon. Precisely because Abidjan is so accessible to them, giving them no impetus to join the exodus from the rural areas to the cities, most Ebrié prefer to live in their villages and to commute to the city. Because the cost of living is lower in the villages, they can have finer houses and more land and lead more relaxed and secure lives among friends and relatives in their villages than they could in Abidjan. Within their village context, the Harrists are indistinguishable in educational level and economic status from other villagers, and there is no difference in the socioeconomic status of villages with different proportions of Harrists, Protestants, and Catholics.

Most Harrist men are farmers, fishermen, brickmasons, or carpenters. Some of the younger literate men are clerks in Abidjan. The educational level of the Harrists, because they are village people, is lower nationally than that of the Protestants and Catholics, who are more highly represented in urban areas where access to western schooling is greatest and most relevant to the life-style. Yet because they live near the capital, where the wealth of the country is concentrated, the Harrists' standard of living is above the national average.

An interesting paradox arose from the prophet's exhortation to his converts to send their children to school to learn to read. Those young men who were sent to school as children, and who would have formed the first generation of western-schooled Harrists, became Catholic or Protestant. In the past the schools available to them were mostly mission schools that mixed religion with education, requiring their students to join the church. Some young men who were brought up in the Harrist church left it upon finishing school to join the Protestant or Catholic church, which they considered to be more fitting to the increased social status with which their schooling had endowed them. The change was also consistent with the European cultural orientation they had learned in school. Other young people, like other members of the modern sector of the Ivorian population, have found that religion has little role in their very secular lives. At present, however, more young people who have gone to school are choosing to remain in the Harrist church because they believe in it as an authentic African institution and expect to play a significant role in its evolution.

The Church and the Village Social System

Some analyses of the phenomenon of African religious innovation stress the function of the contemporary African churches in providing new structures for people who have been uprooted by social change, which is indeed the case in some areas (see, e.g., Mbiti 1970: 306). In such situations these churches provide new bases for a sense of community among people no longer bound by traditional social structures and value systems. In the villages in which Harrist churches are located, the indigenous social structure and value system has largely remained intact, undergoing some modifications, of course, in the process of adapting to the changing larger society, and provides the infrastructure of the Harrist church.

Given this situation, the question arises of what role the Harrist church plays with respect to these indigenous village structures, and how much influence it has on the everyday lives of its members. The best explanation of the situation was furnished by a Harrist minister who said: "In everything that has to do with village life, such as age grade or economic activities, we are villagers. In things that have to do specifically with religion, we are Harrists."

The same situation exists for members of the other churches. The

Catholic and Protestant churches have been superimposed upon the indigenous structures that continue to orient the society. The foreign churches are less congruent with the indigenous structures than the Harrist church because they have continually sought to eliminate certain fundamental institutions, such as the polygamous family. These indigenous political, kinship, and age-grade systems, however, still continue to regulate everyday life and to define people's relationships, obligations, and responsibilities. Church affiliation provides less of a basis for cooperative action than do other structures. Some Harrist leaders, however, are trying to create more collective activities, precisely so that the church will become a more dominant institution in its members' lives.

The different churches do, of course, constitute interest groups, and people sometimes support others on the basis of church membership rather than on the basis of other possible criteria of affiliation. For example, in Abidjan-Santé, because the chief was Protestant, the Harrists believed that his assistant should be a Harrist. And in Abobo-Doumé, three well-situated adjoining house lots were awarded to Harrists by the Harrist villager in charge of distributing the lots. Some Harrists cited this as a reflection of their solidarity and cooperative spirit.

Except in villages where rapport between the churches is poor, members of the same extended, and even nuclear, family—husband, wife, co-wives, siblings, parents, and children—often may belong to different churches. One important Harrist has two brothers who live in his village. One is Catholic and has two Catholic wives, one of them "unofficial." The other brother is a Harrist who has two Harrist wives. The man himself has two wives who are Harrists, and a third who is Catholic. All of his children by the Harrist wives attend the Harrist church, and the Catholic wife has no children yet. One of his sons has a Protestant wife whose father is a minister. To which church will their children belong? According to the husband, whoever goes to church will take them, most probably his wife. When they grow up they will be free to choose for themselves. The two children of one Harrist minister became Catholic because, after going through the western-oriented school system, they rejected their father's church.

There is little difference in actual social practice between Harrists and non-Harrists, even in areas where one might expect it from the differing church doctrines. A prime example is the issue of polygamy. The Harrist church allows polygamy, whereas the Protestant and Catholic churches prohibit it. Protestant and Catholic men, however, often have as many women who are recognized as their wives within the village context, and with whom they have children, as do Harrist men. One prominent and successful young Harrist, for example, has only one wife. In contrast, his best friend, who is Catholic, has one "official" and two generally recognized, but "unofficial," wives. Polygamy is now forbidden by the Ivorian civil code, but on the village level, from the matrimonial perspective, many people behave as if they were Harrists, the indigenous practice prevailing over all newer religious and civil dictates.

Friendship is often a function of church affiliation, although age grade, occupation, and mutual interests are also important determinants of such ties. In villages in which rapport between the churches is poor, membership in a particular church is, as would be expected, a more important determinant of friendship than in villages in which rapport is good. Older Harrists, including ministers and apostles, seem to associate less exclusively with other Harrists than do younger church members. Many of these older people have not been Harrists all of their lives, as the young people have, and therefore did not grow up with other Harrist church members as a potential category from which to choose their friends. The young people who associate primarily with other Harrists share many common interests, such as the choir and other youth activities designed to give them a greater role in the church. Some young Harrists stated that they tend to have more Harrist than non-Harrist friends because "they have the same ideas and are on the right path."

On the level of everyday behavior, neither Harrist nor non-Harrist villagers feel that there are significant behavioral differences between the members of the different churches, precisely because more aspects of their lives are controlled by the social structures shared by all villagers than by church structures. Although the different churches approach them in different ways, the same basic beliefs are shared by most villagers. Because village socioeconomic differences are also not reflected in church membership, church affiliation in itself is not a useful criterion for making social distinctions.

Many non-Harrists express respect for the wisdom, goodness,

and spiritual strength of Harrist ministers, although some add that they would not want to join the Harrist church because it is "too native," meaning that it is deliberately based on indigenous African structures. Such an attitude would seem to indicate that the colonial educational system was quite successful in accomplishing its intention to convince these Ivorians that European cultural forms are by definition superior to their own.

The actual relationships among the various churches depend upon the specific historical events of the village. In Anono, rapport is very good between the Harrists and the Catholics. One Harrist reported that if he missed a Harrist service, he might go to a Catholic mass, and a Catholic friend of his indicated that he sometimes went to Harrist services. In Petit Bassam, in contrast, there is a rivalry between the Harrists and the Protestants that dates back to the early conflict between those villagers who chose to follow the Protestant missionaries and those who, choosing to remain faithful to Harris, encouraged the events that led to John Ahui's visit to Liberia and to the creation of the Harrist church. In Abobo-Doumé, rapport among Harrists, Catholics, and Protestants is good, and marriage frequently occurs between members of the different churches. In some villages the numbers of Harrists are growing, and in some they are declining, a major factor being the vitality of the ministers.

Ideological Differences from the Protestants and Catholics

Although they do not perceive significant day-to-day behavioral differences between themselves and the members of the other churches, the Harrists are very aware of differences on the ideological level. The major difference that many Harrists specify as existing between themselves and the members of the other churches is in the domain of "fetishes." Whereas members of their church cannot have "fetishes" of any sort, because they would be punished by God, neither Protestantism nor Catholicism promises such sanctions. For this reason Harrists consider these other churches hypocritical: "Their members pretend to worship God, but if you look in their pockets you will find something [protective amulets]."

Many Harrists feel that members of the other churches do not have total faith in God because they seek the very kinds of traditional sources of spiritual protection and assistance that Harris condemned. The Catholics are specifically criticized by the Harrists because of the representations of saints in their churches. Harrists consider these statues to be manifestations of idolatry, of the "fetishism" that the Prophet Harris prohibited.

Thus, the Harrists consider themselves spiritually superior to the members of the other churches. They cite as evidence the fact that these others must come to the Harrist church to ask forgiveness for certain serious and frequently occurring sins for which no provisions are made in their own churches, such as witchcraft. The Harrists find the communion services of the Catholics and Protestants shocking and repugnant. To eat the flesh and drink the blood of the son of God symbolically sounds suspiciously like the symbolic eating of flesh and drinking of blood that constitutes witchcraft.

In the years since Independence (1960), with the increased recognition within the missionary Christian churches of the necessity for relating religious forms to the lives of their members, the Protestant and Catholic churches in the Ivory Coast have become increasingly Africanized, both in leadership and in style of worship. African rhythms and instruments are now a part of many church services. On special occasions, other village churches now have processions in the streets like those that characterize the Harrists. The kinds of features for which the Harrists were once disdained have thus been integrated into the Protestant and Catholic churches. Harrists perceive these phenomena as representing an unavowed acknowledgment that they were always right, and as an attempt to attract their members.

Harrists criticize the Ivorians who are members of the Protestant and Catholic churches for wanting to be like Europeans because they belong to European churches rather than to "the church that God sent the Prophet Harris to establish especially for the Ivorians." One Harrist characterized non-Harrists as "people who have no character because they allow others to run their lives." Another said that such people had complexes because they "only think a religion is valid if it is brought by Europeans."

Many Harrists said that all Ivorians should belong to the Harrist church as a manifestation of their integrity as Africans. Older Harrists remember the role of the Catholic church in collaborating with the colonial administration to oppress them and to try to destroy their religion during the decade after Harris's visit. They also recall the pressures on them to attend the Catholic church, which lasted until the 1940s nationalist period when many "white people's Christians" left the colonizers' church for the "religion of the Africans."

For many of the people who left the European churches to join the Harrist church in the 1940s, the move represented an awareness of the desirability of abandoning a religious institution predicated on the destruction of indigenous values and institutions to join one predicated on their preservation. Many Harrists asserted that they prefer the Harrist church because it is based on "an African way of life." According to one person, "What is good about the Harrist religion is that it is realistic. It is based on the realities of African life." René Bureau aptly characterized the Harrist church as "an African institution, controlled by Africans for Africans, responding to African aspirations and needs." (1971: 98).

Harrist Christians?

The Harrists believe that each people was sent its own prophet, and that Jesus was the prophet for the Europeans, whereas Harris was the prophet of the Africans. "The Prophet Harris did the same thing for the Africans that Jesus Christ did for the Europeans —he brought us Christianity. God sent each of his sons to a different group of people to save them. Jesus went to Europe to save the whites, but he did not come to Africa. It was the Prophet Harris, an African like us, whom God sent to bring us into the light." The question may thus arise whether the Harrist church falls within the broad range of religious institutions characterized as Christian. The church doctrine is still evolving, with an increasing emphasis on biblical understanding and interpretation; perhaps the final decision must be left to an African theologian.

The Harrists themselves believe that they are especially privileged Christians because God saw fit to send them their own special messenger. Jesus is commonly depicted as white in the churches introduced by Europeans. The fact that Harris was an African is therefore considered sufficient proof by the Harrists that he was chosen especially for them. Harrists believe that there is only one universal god who is worshiped by different religions in different ways. Thus they believe that the Prophet Harris's god is the same deity worshiped by other Christians, and they also recognize him as their own creator god, whom the Ebrié call Yankan.

There is no question but that Harris set out to convey a Christian message. His vision and sense of mission establish him in the tradition of the biblical prophets. He said that he was "sent by Christ" to "lead back to Christ the lost nations" (van Bulck 1961: 121–22). He urged everyone to "repent and believe in Jesus Christ," saying of himself, "I am his last prophet" (Haliburton 1971: 35). In the message he gave to Pierre Benoit he said, "Everyone must adore the only true God in Jesus Christ, and serve Him alone" (Amos-Djoro 1956: 225). Additionally, Harris told people to call the churches they constructed "Christ Church," and when the Harrist national committee was formed in 1961, it was said to represent the "Church of Christ, Harrist Mission." Songs and sermons in Harrist churches, particularly those with literate ministers, also mention Christ. Harris's intent, like that of the foreign missionaries, was to Christianize.

It is not clear to what extent most Harrists understand the idea, for which their own religious traditions in no way prepared them, of a creator god who sent a flesh-and-blood son to earth to save people, and subsequently allowed this son to be crucified by them. The Harrists, of course, are not alone in Christendom in not finding this concept totally apparent, and the nuances of the issue continue to divide mainstream Euro-Christian denominations. The Ivorians, however, did have a pattern of priests of strong spirits who came to teach people to worship them so as to improve their lives, and they needed to look no further than their own understanding to identify the Prophet Harris as falling within this tradition. They recognized Harris to be different from his predecessors in that he represented not just another strong nature spirit, but the power of the creator god himself.

Whereas Jesus Christ is an abstraction for the Harrists, they or their ancestors actually saw, perhaps were even baptized by, the Prophet Harris. The Harrists recognize Jesus as one of the universal creator god's prophets, as do followers of other religions such as Islam. For many Harrists, Harris and Jesus are viewed in the same way because they played the same role for different peoples. As more ministers make greater use of the Bible, however, there will probably be increased differentiation in the roles of the two messengers of God. As the Harrists become more aware of the role of Jesus in the origin of Christianity, alterations in church doctrine may be expected to occur. For the Bible, rather than himself, to become the ultimate source of authority is exactly what Harris preached as he told his converts to seek the Word of God in the Holy Book.

The Harrists in the Nation

In the Ivory Coast the status and image of the Harrist church are somewhat ambiguous. The 1955 census of the Commune of Abidjan listed the Harrists as a separate Christian religious group, along with the Catholics, Protestants, and "other Christians"; other categories were Muslims, Animists, "other religions," and "no religion." The Harrists were also listed as a category in the 1958 census of Bouaké, the nation's second largest city, although the Harrists in Bouaké numbered only 7 out of 42,498 people (Recensement d'Abidjan 1955: 29; Recensement Démographique de Bouaké 1958: 19).

In contrast, the 1966 *Annuaire Nationale de la Côte d'Ivoire* listed the national religions as Muslim, Catholic, and Protestant, although in 1964 the government political party had acknowledged the Harrists as constituting the fourth national religion. The *Annuaire* described the Protestant, meaning almost exclusively Methodist, sphere of influence as the entire southeast of the country (Annuaire nationale de la Côte d'Ivoire 1966: 101–7). The described area is coterminous with that in which the Harrist church has its greatest influence. No mention was made of the Harrists, however, although they are more numerous, better known, and more significant in the nation than the small Protestant groups listed.

The official position of the Ivorian government toward the Harrist church is favorable because of the government's positive stance toward organized religion. According to August Denise, minister of state and acting president during President Houphouet-Boigny's absence:

The government encourages religion in the Ivory Coast.
We members of the government feel that religion is important to
the development of the country because it gives people the moral
background to make them behave as they should. Many of us
are appalled at the moral decadence and the lack of faith in anything but materialism that one finds in the developed countries.
We feel that such a situation would hinder the development of
the Ivory Coast. There would be nothing to prevent people from
committing crimes and otherwise misbehaving. Therefore, we
try to avoid the influence of absolute materialism by encouraging
religion on all levels of the society.

The animists, for example, are afraid to do wrong because they
fear their gods and fetishes. But with modernization many people
are losing faith in such traditional things. Therefore, the government encourages all churches, but does not give favoritism
to any one. As far as the government is concerned, the Harrist
religion is as important as the others since some people who will
not become Protestant or Catholic for various reasons will be
attracted to the Harrist church. [Personal interview, 3 August
1972]

In 1964, the government political party, the Parti Démocratique
de la Côte d'Ivoire (PDCI), decided to encourage the national religions actively by sponsoring a drive to collect money to build a
religious edifice for each one along the proposed Voie Triomphale
in downtown Abidjan. Contributions were made by the president
and other political and governmental officials. The party was responsible for seeing that funds were collected from everyone in the
country. Local government officials acted as the collection agents in
this drive, which was a part of PDCI activities for three years. The
initial intention was to build three religious edificies—one each for
the Catholics, Protestants, and Muslims.

Although President Houphouet-Boigny had praised the work of
the Prophet Harris in leading multitudes of people from their traditional religious practices to Christianity, the Harrist church was
considered by most Ivorians, including most members of the government, to be only a "religion of old men"; it was not taken seriously as a major Ivorian religious institution. This exclusion from
the roster of national religions of what they considered to be the

only authentically Ivorian religion sparked the Harrists to action. The Harrist national committee succeeded in convincing the PDCI that their church was indeed a dynamic institution that should be recognized as such. Harrist churches made significant contributions to the construction fund. Although neither the Voie Triomphale nor the buildings has yet been begun, the Harrists were pleased to be accorded governmental recognition of what they see as their rightful place in the nation's religious life.

On state occasions such as the annual Independence celebration or the official visit of an important foreign dignitary, John Ahui, as leader of the Harrist church, is invited to attend along with other religious, civic, and popular leaders—to represent part of the diverse human constituency of the Ivory Coast. When President Senghor of Senegal made his historic visit to the Ivory Coast in 1971, for example, Ahui was present to greet him.

The Harrists' Popular Image

The popular image of the Harrists is generally quite uninformed or misinformed. Most people in the southern coastal area know that the Harrists exist, usually because they have happened upon a procession to or from a Harrist church service, or because they know about the Harrist New Year's Eve, All Saints' Day, or Rain Feast celebrations. Most people who are not members of the ethnic groups in which the Harrists are numerically significant, however, know little about them other than that they dress in white and have processions. Members of the western educated elite tend to consider them folkloric and picturesque. The local media has unfortunately contributed to perpetuating misinformation about the Harrist church.

The national weekend magazine *Ivoire Dimanche* printed in 1971 a feature article entitled "The Disciples of William Harris" (Koffi 1971). The article consisted of an interview with one of the Harrist ministers with a cane and a general description of the religion. Both parts of the article contained a number of blatant errors, including the names of both the interviewee and the village where the interview took place, errors that irate Harrist readers pointed out in letters to the editor in subsequent issues of the magazine. The Harrists were particularly angered by the appearance of this article portraying them as primitive, picturesque, folkloric, and a good tourist attraction at a time when they were making special efforts to adapt their church to contemporary realities.

After underestimating the geographical area in which the Harrist churches are found and the number of ethnic groups involved, this article stated:

> The Harrist religion is without a doubt interesting. It has a Christian base, but a Christianity that is profoundly altered and adapted.
>
> Of course, the true Christians consider the Harrists with suspicion, even with real hostility. And a good number of Christians must regret the fact that the time no longer exists when this sect would have been pursued as heretical and prohibited. In fact, if one takes the point of view of Christian orthodoxy, it is difficult not to think of the Harrist religion that which a reflective person said of a monkey in comparison to a man. "A disgrace and an object of derision." Wouldn't that be excessive? [P. 5]

The author, Yao Koffi, went on to describe the positive aspects of the Harrist church. Having acknowledged that "the Christian religion is sad," with its "solemn rites" and an atmosphere in which "joy is looked upon with suspicion," Koffi stated paternalistically:

> However, the Harrist religion is a religion profoundly adapted to the mentality and the degree of civilization of the Ivorians of 1895.[2] It is gay, simple, and puts together agreeably music, dance, and religion. The austerity, the aesceticism and the general elevation of the Christian religion are suitable for men who have attained a high level of spiritual development. Look at the Harrists. When they come out of the church they dance as people have always danced in the villages. In singing the songs as people have always sung them, only the words have changed.
>
> As one can see, the Harrist sect could better succeed in implanting itself than the pure and hard religion, of which it was just the vulgarization. As a matter of fact, isn't that the way it always is? When it is necessary to descend to the level of the masses, it is indispensable to abandon certain aristocratic values. [Pp. 4–5]

After presenting the interview, in which the minister sketched the history and organization of the church, said that Harrists used the Protestant Bible, and described the way in which some ministers cured people through the use of confession and prayer, Koffi concluded: "There it is. As one can see, the Harrist religion is really far from Christianity. But can one deny that it is, in its own way, a religion?" (p. 6).

Two major Harrist celebrations, the Rain Feast in Petit Bassam and the All Saints' Day celebration in Bregbo, often merit brief articles in the daily newspaper, and both have been televised on programs portraying Ivorian folklore, art, and traditions. Harrist choirs have also sung on the radio on Sundays. In addition, important Harrist events, such as the dedication of a new church or a significant meeting, may be reported in the daily newspaper as local news or human interest items. Thus, after the August 1972 Congress of Young Harrist Intellectuals, the national daily paper, *Fraternité-Matin*, ran an article entitled "The Harrist Religion Wants to Adapt Itself to the Realities of the Twentieth Century" (5 September 1972: 7). The article indicated some of the changes proposed by conference participants in what it termed the Harrists' "medieval practices," while recognizing that the philosophical basis of the religion was sufficiently serious for the Harrist church to have been recognized as a national religion in 1964.

In 1972 there was a television special on the activities of Harrist healer Albert Atcho,[3] in the village of Bregbo. Viewers with no prior preparation or further information about the Harrists saw people confess to "being devils"; to having killed family members, friends, and neighbors "as a devil"; and to having "eaten people's flesh and drunk their blood." Although the commentator briefly explained the symbolic meaning of the phenomenon in question, many viewers found the show shocking and did not understand that all of the cannibalism discussed was "at a distance." They were convinced that Bregbo was an evil place, and when they were made aware of Atcho's position as a prominent Harrist, concluded that the Harrist church was a diabolical phenomenon. One well-educated Harrist, commenting favorably on Atcho's work in Bregbo, expressed his regret that, because this aspect of the Harrist church is one that draws a great deal of attention, but about which most people are severely misinformed, it tends to give people a very inaccurate image of the Harrists.

Many enlightened Ivorians who are interested in their national culture have a great deal of respect for the Harrist church and what it represents. One very prominent political figure said of those people who scorn the Harrist church: "Their attitudes are a manifestation of their own intellectual alienation, in that they only want to identify with those things that were brought by the colonizers." In his opinion, they should respect the Harrist religion as a form of Christianity that has become, by virtue of being adapted to the indigenous way of life, an authentically African religion.

CHAPTER 8
Harrist Beliefs and Doctrine

As the Harrist movement developed into the Harrist church, leaders of the new institution proceeded with two tasks: adapting the prophet's teaching to contemporary realities, and creating a doctrine that would replace the traditional one in responding to the concerns of everyday life. The translation of the prophet's teachings from the realm of the ideal to the vicissitudes of the real world necessarily entailed modifications. During the course of the development of the church, Harrist leaders extrapolated upon the prophet's teachings in order to respond to aspects of life about which he had not provided guidance. Harris's teachings provided an outline to be filled with elements of the indigenous culture in interaction with responses to the sociopolitical milieu, all interpreted or reinterpreted in accordance with the themes of the prophet's message.

As the prophetic movement developed into a church, the focus changed. The fundamental goal of Harris's message had been accomplished. He had urged people to hurry to become Christians because the time was rapidly approaching when all nonbelievers would be destroyed. The goal of effecting this theological revolution had been achieved as the multitudes who encountered the prophet became Christians. The task of defining the content of their version of Christianity rested with the leaders of the Harrist church. A doctrine had to be created to explain the converts' new relationship to their god and to their social reality.

Salvation and Prosperity

The Harrists believe that God sent Harris to bring them happiness by helping them to live better lives on earth. The content of such happiness is found in Harrist prayers, which have as their major themes the traditional desires for many children, good health, success in farming or fishing, a well-paying job if they work in the city, general prosperity, and protection from ill fortune. If people serve God faithfully, they have reason to hope that their prayers will be answered. Harrists say that during the prophet's mission of conversion, immediate prosperity, in the form of abundant catches of fish, bountiful harvests, radiant good health, and the like, were the fruits of beginning to worship Harris's god. Immediate punishment, in the form of empty fishnets, scant harvests, illness, and premature deaths, awaited those who refused to heed the prophet's message. Consequently, people who prosper are considered to be living proof that those who worship God correctly benefit from his grace.

The Harrists attribute their improved standard of living since the period when Harris came to the fact that they did learn to worship God as he taught them. John Ahui and other Harrist leaders are convinced that the progress they see in the Ivory Coast today and the materially better life the Ivorians live now are clear indexes of the veracity of the prophet's message. Some Harrists say that with Harris's teachings, the "spirit of development" entered the country, allowing people to succeed in their undertakings. Before Harris's arrival they had been "controlled by the devil," who did not want them to live well and who did not want the country to develop. There are also prominent non-Harrists who share the conviction that the teachings and effects of the Prophet Harris had a profound positive influence on all of the people he touched, not just on those who became Harrists.

Harrists feel that Harris's prophecies have largely been fulfilled. They cite persuasive examples, such as the fact that before the prophet came few Ivorians knew how to read and write. He told them to send their children to school: there are now schools in most villages, and most younger Harrists are literate. Another example frequently cited is Harris's statement that if his converts worshiped as he taught for seven years they could live in western-style houses.

Harrists compare the sometimes several-storied concrete houses in their villages with the mud brick houses found in villages farther north where Harris's message did not penetrate, as further evidence of the realization of the prophet's predictions. In addition, according to the Harrists, the prophet promised that a "son of Africa" would one day rule the nation: they see this prophecy fulfilled in the person of President Félix Houphouet-Boigny.

Although the Harrists contend that their lives improved markedly as the result of Harris's influence, they realize that life is not perfect and that evil does continue to exist. A statement made by healer Albert Atcho to a group of non-Harrists who had come to his village to be healed concisely expresses the Harrists' explanation of the significance of what the prophet did for them. It also explains why life is not as ideal as it should be: most people failed to live up to the prophet's teachings.

> Why did God send Harris? He sent him because of your suffering and for your happiness. Your happiness is religion, education, intelligence. And Harris also burned your fetishes. He brought the cross and baptism to wash away your sins. Before him, who among the Africans knew how to worship God? Who knew how to pray? Before him who knew reading and writing from being educated, who among us Africans knew how to work in an office? No one. . . . And nevertheless today Harris has no name with you, nor does his religion. After following him for three years you returned to your former customs: devils, fetishes, [sacred] swamps, witches. And you also have religions that do not belong to you: you have chosen foreign religions. Don't you know that all of the happiness you ask of God goes to whites, and you get nothing? If you had worshiped God for seven years as the Prophet Harris said, God would be pleased with you. [Bureau 1971: 164]

The prophet saved his converts by baptizing them, by purifying, protecting, and forgiving them for their sins. He offered them the promise of an improvement in their lives if they would worship his god faithfully. He further admonished them to seek and acquire what he regarded as a major tool of progress—education. Unfortunately, many of his converts did not remain faithful to Harris's teachings for the seven-year period he stipulated because of persecution by the colonial administration. Many people wrongfully, according to Harrist doctrine, joined missionary churches. Only a few of Harris's converts practiced his religion continuously. Most of the older people who are currently Harrists had abandoned the prophet's teachings at some point, and resumed practicing them only during the 1940s' wave of reconversion.

As they witness the continuing discrepancies in material well-being between themselves and the Europeans, the Harrists acknowledge their own responsibility for having failed to keep the prophet's mandate. Had Harris's converts continued to worship as he told them, they could, they believe, have already achieved everything the Europeans have. They could have the same "mentality, power, and luck" as the Europeans and they would be able to do everything they do, "such as make airplanes."

Because they did not completely fulfill Harris's demands, however, the Ivorians have not yet received all of the promised benefits. They still have not obtained the Europeans' level of knowledge and technology, and they must continue to work hard and pray to God in order to attain the materially and spiritually advanced state they would have already reached had they been faithful to Harris for the required time. Just as their disobedient ancestors had spoiled their good lives under the care of their creator god, the Ivorians, again through their own fault, had missed a second opportunity to lead prosperous lives free of misfortune.

Beyond Conversion

Harris's converts initially held the utopian belief that the prophet's god would solve all of their problems. Harris was believed to have created the condition for the elimination of evil by exhibiting the superior power of his god over those forces that could be invoked by people who sought to harm others. His baptism was believed to purify people of past sins and prohibit them from sinning in the future. Protected by a stronger power, people were free to rid themselves of the religious objects housing the spirits to whom they had previously looked for protection from evil, as well as to defy traditional taboos. The oral tradition tells glorious stories about what happened when entire villages began to worship the Christian god: no one died in one village for several years; more than one hundred children were born in one year in another village where previously only two or three children had been born annually; people were even raised from the dead.

Consequently, the expectation developed that, with the worship of the Christian god, all misfortune would cease to exist. The creator god who had once assured his children a wonderful life would do so again, now that they had returned to his worship. The only way to suffer misfortune in the future, they reasoned, was to incur the wrath of this powerful god, should they fail to manifest their exclusive faith in him. This was the reason the Harrist Protestants were so anxious for teachers to come to help them to become proper Christians.

Unfortunately, although there was no longer any reason for evil and misfortune to exist, even in the villages in which life was reported to have been idyllic after the villagers' conversion to Christianity the state of paradise lasted only temporarily. Even though God cared for his creatures, who were now worshiping him correctly, evil and misfortune were again found to exist. The Harrists were not the first members of a new religion to experience such disappointment. The surviving religions of the world are those that have found a sufficiently satisfying way of explaining the persistence of evil and misfortune in a world that should have been made perfect by the faith of the worshipers.

The Harrists found the explanation to this problematic situation in the notion that, although people might seem to worship God properly, they continued to sin against one another through the medium of witchcraft, the destructive use of spiritual force that results in human misfortune. Consequently, even though it does not appear to be a major issue in the prophet's teachings (although he clearly acknowledged it as a problem), the concept of witchcraft occupies a position of importance in present-day Harrist thought.

Harrist sermons and songs emphasize that although Harris came to save the Africans from sin, and although they pretend to be good Christians by praying to God with great frequency, most people continue to sin. As one Harrist minister stated, "Good progresses one step and then stops and rests. Evil progresses at one hundred kilometers an hour." Bureau quotes Albert Atcho as saying, "I tell you, there isn't an African who has only done good acts from morning to evening; there isn't one in the world. We are always evil doers, we commit sins each time; we must pray to God all the time to ask him to pardon our sins" (1971: 154). Church members are frequently warned that if they continue to sin they will be punished. This emphasis on people's sinful nature is not, of course, unique to the Harrists, nor are the Harrists alone among Ivorian Christians in defining evil in terms of the symbolic language of witchcraft.[1] The Harrist church, as an institution predicated on the indigenous world view, is, however, the only Christian church in the Ivory Coast that openly acknowledges witchcraft as a problem and formally deals with it.

Monica Wilson's 1971 account of a conversation with a Nyakyusa woman in southern Africa provides an enlightening explanation of the meaning of witchcraft in Africa. The Nyakyusa woman asked Wilson to tell her the truth about witchcraft among Europeans. Wilson responded that few whites believed in witchcraft. The Nyakyusa woman said that Wilson's answer was the same as that of other whites who, she believed, refused to admit the truth. In her opinion, it was impossible that there could be a society without witchcraft.

The woman's assertion led Wilson to think about the meaning of the term for witchcraft in the Nyakyusa language, which, she realized, translated into English simply as "evildoing." By denying that witchcraft existed in Europe, Wilson was denying that ill will, hatred, and greed existed there. She concluded that "the idea of witchcraft acknowledges the reality of evil: the denial of it is taken as a denial of the existence of evil." Africans are aware of evil impulses, of lust, greed, and envy, in themselves. They therefore assume that they exist also in others. They cannot believe that any society exists without such feelings, which they understand to be made evident in the practice of witchcraft. A belief in witchcraft, therefore, provides an explanation for good and ill fortune. If one suffers, it is because of the ill will of an enemy (Wilson 1971: 36–39).

If You Do Good . . .

In the Harrist church there has been a significant conceptual change in the locus of responsibility for good and evil and in the individual's sense of control over her or his own fate.[2] Because prosperity is a manifestation of God's pleasure, people should be free to exercise their ambitions and to enjoy the fruits of their efforts without fear of being harmed. Whereas, in the past, success was often the result of harming someone else, it is now the result of personal effort and of worshiping God. This new attitude is concisely expressed in the inscription in the Harrist church in the Dida village of Abatou-Lilié:

> If you do good, it is for you.
> If you do evil, it is for you.

Thus, just as the creator god punished the Africans for their evil-doing by allowing the Europeans to conquer them, he punishes individuals for using their spiritual force to harm others. The evildoer will suffer, not the potential victim. People are responsible for their good fortune as well as for their misfortunes, and a person should seek the source of personal misfortune not in others, but in his or her own dubious motives. "God gives people everything to be happy. If people aren't happy, it is their own fault because they seek riches by means other than those God provides." Because evil and misfortune come from oneself rather than from others, one should not need to fear being attacked by jealous neighbors.

As in other religions, however, the system is imperfect. Innocent people still suffer, and some people who seem to be evil prosper. God is supposed to punish people for their sins and make the perpetrators of wickedness pay for their doings. Yet despite the protection a person may get from frequent prayer, the victim of another's aggression may still suffer misfortune, become ill, or die. In fact, the misfortune, illness, or death of a villager who is considered innocent of sin will often provide the impetus for seeking the confession of someone known to harbor ill will for the victim. Yet, in general, as in other religions, the Harrists affirm their doctrinal ideal, viewing personal misfortune as the result of one's own evil intentions and prosperity as the reward for being a good Christian, while recognizing pragmatically that this ideal is never attained.

Spiritual Force and Contemporary Society

Extrapolating from their explanation of differences in fortune within their own society, the Harrists' belief system accounts for the continuing discrepancy in levels of prosperity between the Africans and the Europeans who conquered them on the basis of the indigenous concept of spiritual force. In Harrist doctrine all of God's creatures have the same quantity of spiritual force, which is fundamentally amoral in character.[3] Inasmuch as there is no difference in the quantity or moral quality of the spiritual force of different people, it is the use to which they put it that determines its effects. This force can be used positively or negatively, constructively or destructively. The Harrists believe that the Europeans' greater technological knowledge and power result from the difference in use that the two groups make of their spiritual force rather than from any difference in their inherent potential. One Harrist said, "Europeans don't have twenty fingers or forty toes to make them superior." Another said, "Whatever Europeans do, Africans can also learn to do without their help. Africans lack the means at present, but with patience we can expect to succeed. It is only ignorance that makes some Africans think they need Europeans to help them. One day, Africans won't say that any longer."

According to the Harrists, the Europeans have more knowledge and are more prosperous than the Africans because the Europeans, as a group, use their spiritual force in a positive manner—simply because they have been Christian longer. Because "Jesus taught the Europeans about God before the Prophet Harris came to teach us Ivorians how to worship him," the Europeans have known how to direct their spiritual energies toward doing good rather than evil for a longer time, which explains their material advancement. Speaking of the period before Harris came, one Harrist said, "In the old days everything was bad. People lived in fear because other people who were jealous of what they had would try to harm them. The old people had a lot of spiritual force—more than people have now—but instead of using it for good, they used it to do evil."

Harrists also recognize that the current inequality between Europeans and Africans did not always exist. Their own ancestors had been powerful and sovereign, but they had misused their spiritual force. Consequently, God had punished them by allowing the whites to conquer them. "In the past Africans were dominant, but their spirits were too evil. The kings took justice into their own hands as if they were God. They would kill people who did things that they didn't like. So, to punish the Africans, the whites became dominant. But now their reign is coming to an end. Whether the Africans will oppress the Europeans like the Europeans did our ancestors remains to be seen." Thus, because of their misuse of their spiritual force, the Africans are responsible for their present state. Harris provided the turning point. He taught the Ivorians the means of redressing their wrongs, showing them how to direct their spiritual force in a positive manner.

Harrists illustrate the difference in the uses that Europeans and Africans make of the same spiritual force by citing the example of a man who wants to build a pretty new house for himself in his village. If an African tries to build such a house, his neighbors will become jealous and try to harm him through witchcraft.[4]

In contrast, Harrists say that if a European builds a pretty new house, his neighbor may also be envious; but rather than trying to retaliate by harming him through witchcraft, the neighbor will try to build an even better house next door. Thus, Harrists conclude, "Whereas the Africans have the spirit of evil, the Europeans have the spirit of development." Whereas the Ivorians use their spiritual force to spoil their neighbor's harvest, the Europeans use theirs to build skyscrapers and airplanes. Consequently, if the Africans begin to use their spiritual force constructively, as the Europeans do, they will be able to know, have, and do the same things as the Europeans, just as Harris promised.

A major goal of the Harrist church today, then, is to convince its members to use their spiritual force for constructive rather than destructive purposes so that people may be free and safe to develop their full potential. By using their spiritual force positively, people should experience prosperity in all aspects of their lives, because the force that in the past was used to cause misfortune would now cause prosperity. If people would adhere faithfully to the doctrine of the Harrist church, evil would finally cease to exist.

Accounts of Harris's teachings do not mention any such specific formulation about the nature and uses of spiritual force. Instead, the

Harrist concept appears to be a synthesis of ideas composed of elements of the prophet's dicta concerning the equality of God's creatures, rewards for faithful worship, and traditional concepts about spiritual force and the nature of evil. The development of the new formulation of spiritual force arose when the Harrists found it necessary to account for power and knowledge differences between themselves and the Europeans who had subjugated them.

The traditional concept of spiritual force and its evil manifestation in the form of witchcraft had accounted for the vicissitudes of power, wealth, prosperity, and misfortune within the lagoons societies. The imposition of European dominance caused important changes in these societies that affected those same social dynamics. Such fundamental social changes required an explanation. Because the Europeans manifested superior wealth and power, they might have been described as having superior spiritual force.

It is likely that in the trauma of the colonial situation the Harrists initially explained the European conquest by positing that the Europeans had greater spiritual force than the Africans, as evidenced by their technological accomplishments. The change to the present concept would logically have taken place at a time when the Ivorians found themselves in a position to challenge any notions of European superiority.

World War II made important contributions to the growth of political nationalism in Africa. The Africans witnessed the fallibility of the European troops and their dependence on African human and material aid. They also learned new technical skills; and most important, from their experiences fighting around the globe in the armies of the colonial powers, they gained a broader perspective on world affairs and on the relationships between the colonizers and the colonized. As a result of this exposure, they were no longer willing to accept the oppressive colonial status quo when they returned home from the war (J. Harris 1971: 186).

The sociopolitical environment of the nationalist period during which the Harrist church expanded and became institutionalized provided the proper context for a doctrinal change in the Harrists' way of accounting for the inequality of technological advancement between Africans and Europeans. Africans began to meet Europeans on equal footing and to lead other Africans in opposition to the Europeans. An interpretation consistent with the new state of affairs was that both Europeans and Africans had been created with the same amount of spiritual force by their common Christian god. The difference in their degrees of material advancement and progress lay only in their respective uses of this spiritual force. Consequently, the Africans had the same potential for achievement as did the Europeans.

This reformulation is consistent with Harris's teachings that the Ivorians could acquire the same knowledge as the Europeans if they became Christians. It was not, however, until the nationalist period that the Harrists could begin to actualize this element of the prophet's message, and thus have the proof of their own equal spiritual abilities. Henceforth, the Harrists began to believe that Africans could effectively redress the oppressiveness of the colonial situation by redirecting the use of their spiritual force from evil to good.

Lest the Ivorians' evaluation of themselves as prone to destructive behavior make them appear too aberrant, it is essential to remember that the witchcraft of which they speak is purely symbolic. Their cannibalism is at a distance, not a physical act. And lest their evaluation of the reasons for the technological superiority of the western societies suggest that these societies are in any way morally superior to that of the Ivorians, an incident from the United States about an Afro-American man's attempt to build a nice brick house for his family is particularly relevant, because Harrists often cite the same example in distinguishing between destructive African behavior and constructive European behavior in accounting for the different levels of material development of the two societies:

> My uncle and his wife worked very hard and built themselves a beautiful brick home—on his own property, now. It was brick and a lot of the whites didn't have brick, just the very rich. But he built him a nice brick home. Now, every time he built this home it got burned down while he was at church. No one knew why. They had not left any fire. But three times he built it up and three times they burned it down to the ground. Then after that he built a wooden one and it stayed. No one bothered it. You see, the white community was the [Ku Klux] Klan. Nobody ever told him that his house was too grand; they figured that he should have sense enough to know that. . . . I guess the white people

didn't want the black people to have anything that showed prosperity because a lot of them didn't have it themselves. They had the best of what was available for themselves and their kids, but still they wanted someone to lord it over. I guess they wanted to keep him down. [Gwaltney 1980: 275]

The experience of this Afro-American man in the American South is only one of many that could be cited to suggest that the material advancement of European, and in this case Euro-American, Christians is often not a result of their constructive use of their spiritual force, but rather the result of the destructive use of their physical force against other people.

The Ivorian villagers are not sufficiently exposed to such foreign realities to be aware that the jealousy of the prosperity of another person would lead people in a technologically advanced nation not only to wish the person ill, but also to destroy the person's property physically and even take his or her life. According to the Harrist world view, it is consistent for them to assume that the prosperity of the technological societies results from the constructive use of their spiritual force, and hence from God's blessings. Their experiences and knowledge of the world are not sufficiently broad to allow them to realize that much of this prosperity is based on the exploitation of others and on the destruction or appropriation not only of their property, but also of their cultures and their very lives. Although fully aware of their own suffering at the hands of the French, the Harrists are not aware that they themselves are victims of a worldwide process of European and U.S. imperialism that led to the advancement of the western societies through the exploitation and oppression of many non-Western, nonwhite peoples very much like themselves.

Hence, there is an irony in the Harrists' world view that becomes apparent when they are situated within the broader picture of the larger colonial process. The Harrists see their own evil as the source of their lack of progress. This evil, however, is expressed only symbolically, by wishing people evil, by "cannibalism at a distance." Their models for correct behavior are the members of that very European society which deprived the Ivorians of their sovereignty; tried to destroy their culture through French education, religion, and military force; attacked their villages and exiled their leaders;

and obliged them to do forced labor for the economic benefit of France. The evil of the Ivorians is expressed in the symbolic and abstract form of witchcraft. That of the Europeans has been, on the contrary, concrete and immediate.

CHAPTER 9

From Prophetic Movement
to African Christian Church

From Harrist Movement to Harrist Church

Two distinct stages stand out in the development of the Harrist church: (1) the proselytizing period during which the Prophet Harris strove to fulfill his divine mission of converting people from their old religion to the promise of a new one, and (2) the organizational period during which John Ahui and his assistants developed a church structure and doctrine that would operationalize the prophet's teachings.

In the first stage, Harris's task was to convey a new message that would reorient his converts' thinking and behavior. In the second stage, Ahui was charged with the task of creating an apparatus for the implementation of this message. In the proselytizing period, Harris exhorted people to become Christians. In the organizational period, Ahui created a structure in which they could be Christians in a way compatible with their indigenous culture.

These two stages may be further divided into four developmental phases:

Phase one (1913–14) was the period of the religious revolution during which Harris converted masses of worshipers of the indigenous spirits to the worship of the Christian god. Imparting to them a rudimentary knowledge of Christianity, he instructed them to worship the Christian god: by joining the Catholic church, by seeking instruction from his designated disciples, or by building their own houses of prayer in which to worship while they awaited teachers who would come to help them.

145

Evolution of the Harrist Church

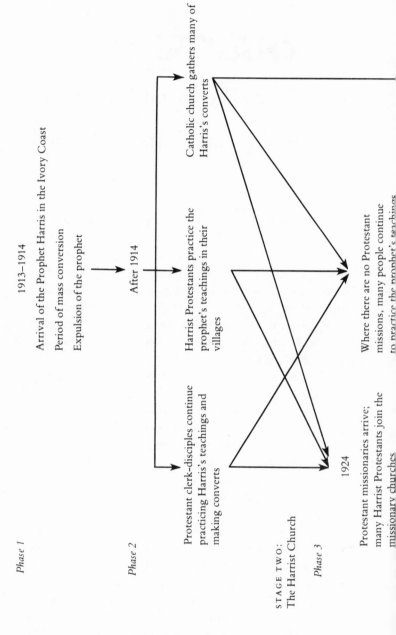

STAGE ONE:
The Harrist Movement

Phase 1

1913–1914

Arrival of the Prophet Harris in the Ivory Coast

Period of mass conversion

Expulsion of the prophet

Phase 2

After 1914

Protestant clerk-disciples continue practicing Harris's teachings and making converts

Harrist Protestants practice the prophet's teachings in their villages

Catholic church gathers many of Harris's converts

STAGE TWO:
The Harrist Church

Phase 3

1924

Protestant missionaries arrive; many Harrist Protestants join the missionary churches

Where there are no Protestant missions, many people continue to practice the prophet's teachings

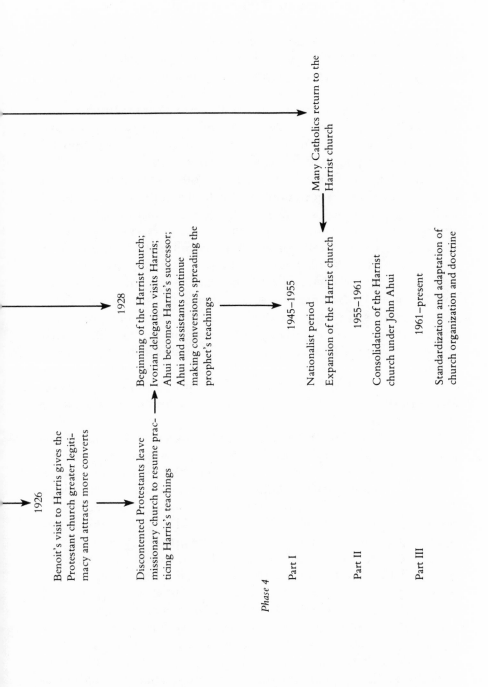

1926

Benoit's visit to Harris gives the Protestant church greater legitimacy and attracts more converts

Discontented Protestants leave missionary church to resume practicing Harris's teachings

1928

Beginning of the Harrist church; Ivorian delegation visits Harris; Ahui becomes Harris's successor, Ahui and assistants continue making conversions, spreading the prophet's teachings

Many Catholics return to the Harrist church

Phase 4

Part I
1945–1955
Nationalist period
Expansion of the Harrist church

Part II
1955–1961
Consolidation of the Harrist church under John Ahui

Part III
1961–present
Standardization and adaptation of church organization and doctrine

The content of Harris's teachings was determined by his experiences in Liberia: his educational and religious background, his work as a lay evangelist and interpreter, his political experiences and material life-style, his own understanding of the Bible, and the influence of ideological leaders such as Edward Wilmot Blyden. The religion he taught combined elements of his Protestant missionary training, aspects of the indigenous belief system, and a pragmatic program for coping with the reality of colonialism.

Harris won the favor of the French colonial administration with his missionarylike exhortations to work diligently, obey temporal authority, and avoid excessive drinking. He won the favor of the Ivorians by combining a compelling message about a powerful supreme god who would protect them from evil and bring them prosperity with a familiar form of presentation reminiscent of indigenous religious behaviors.[1] The Ivorians were particularly receptive because Harris came at a time when their assumptions about and techniques for assuring their own prosperity and protection from misfortune were proving inadequate in the face of French colonial demands. In addition, the prophet threatened dire consequences to those who did not heed his message, whereas he promised immediate benefits to those who did. Furthermore, he provided awe-inspiring proof of the validity of his contentions, thus securing mass conversions.

Phase two (1915–24) was the period between the prophet's departure from the Ivory Coast and the arrival of the Protestant missionaries. Harris's converts tried to obey his message in various ways—by joining the Catholic church or by practicing his teachings alone or with the help of the Methodist clerk-disciples. For those people who tried to continue to practice Harris's teachings, this phase, beginning with the expulsion of the prophet, was characterized by religious persecution at the hands of the colonial administration, aided by the Catholic missionaries. The clerk-disciples were forbidden to preach and some were jailed. Those people who tried to remain faithful to the Prophet Harris, and who refused to join the Catholic mission, found it necessary to worship in secret.

In their clandestine worship, the prophet's faithful began to synthesize the beliefs and practices that the prophet had taught them with congruent elements of their indigenous religion. Traditional priests became ministers of the new religion, and the older men who had had so much power in the indigenous societies became apostles and elders. People worshiped the new god with music similar to that which they had used in the worship of the traditional spirits. Thus, basic social institutions and practices remained largely unchallenged. This period of clandestine religious autonomy paved the way for the assertion of Ivorian religious initiative that took place in the third phase.

Phase three (1924–45) was characterized by three occurrences: the arrival of the Protestant missionaries whom Harrist Protestants believed to be the teachers with Bibles the prophet had told them would come; the visits of Pierre Benoit and John Ahui to Liberia to seek approval from the prophet for their respective religious orientations; and the beginning of a new and autonomous religious institution.

The opening event of this phase was the arrival, in 1924, of the Protestant missionaries and their discovery of the tens of thousands of Harrist Protestants eagerly waiting to learn to become good Christians. Many Ivorians joined the Protestants and were confirmed in their decision by Harris's message to his converts, brought back from Liberia by Pierre Benoit in 1926.

Some of these people, however, having already practiced their own version of Harris's Christianity for ten years, found the demands of the Protestant missionaries contrary to their expectations. The foreigners required changes in fundamental indigenous social institutions as a condition for church membership and insisted upon usurping the authority of the village leaders whom Harris had charged with implementing his teachings. The missionaries also instituted church practices incongruous with the prophet's message and actions. Consequently, an Ivorian delegation was sent to ask the prophet's advice about how to proceed.

The Ivorian delegation's visit to Harris in 1928 ushered in part two of the third phase and provided the impetus for the creation of the Harrist church. Thereafter, Ahui and his disciples began creating a religious organization with a structure, a doctrine, and a set of practices that were an amalgam of the indigenous social structure and belief system, Christian practices, and Harris's teachings, each modified in adaptation to the others.

Phase four (from 1945 on), which is divisible into three parts, began with the onset of the nationalist period. This phase was characterized by the expansion and consolidation of the church and by efforts to standardize and codify its doctrine and practices and adapt them to contemporary realities. Part one of phase four coincided with the nationalist period of the second half of the 1940s and first half of the 1950s, during which there was a great influx of the prophet's original converts back to the Harrist church.

The 1944 Conference of Brazzaville sowed the seeds for the eventual political independence of France's overseas colonies, allowing for the creation of political parties and labor unions there. In 1945 the Parti Démocratique de la Côte d'Ivoire (PDCI) was organized by Félix Houphouet-Boigny; this organization led to the development of the regional Rassemblement Démocratique Africain (RDA) in 1946 for all of French West Africa. The leaders of these organizations called upon their people to struggle against colonialism. During this period, Harrist churches sprang up in many villages as Ivorians rejected the missionary churches, particularly the Catholic church, because of its association with the oppressive colonial administration, in favor of what they called the "religion of the Africans." After three long decades of unrelenting persecution, the people who had been trying to maintain the religion of the Prophet Harris clandestinely could again do so freely and openly.

The great influx of members seeking a new religious orientation caused church leaders to begin to articulate and define directions the church should take, and to propose programs to make these ideas a reality. Part two of this phase, then, consisted of the process of consolidating the groups that considered themselves Harrists into a cohesive body under unitary leadership. This period was highlighted by the 1955 Petit Bassam conference.

Part three, beginning with national independence in 1960, continues to be characterized by efforts inspired by younger, progressive church leaders to standardize church doctrine and practice and to take steps to adapt them to the context of contemporary Ivorian life.

A Man of Destiny

William Wade Harris was unquestionably an outstanding personage of his era. He was known as a religious leader in four

African countries as well as in missionary circles in England and
France. Such renown was a phenomenal accomplishment for anyone, but especially for an African of limited western schooling and
obscure parentage. He authored an unprecedented and unique
movement of mass conversion to Christianity on the African continent, which revolutionized the religious lives of more than a
hundred thousand people. Harris's ministry also led to the success of
two European Christian missionary endeavors, and to the growth
of other important West African religious movements.

A number of experiential factors prepared Harris to assume the
role of religious innovator. His background was significantly different from that of his Ivorian converts. He had grown up partially in
a traditional setting and partially in a Christian Protestant setting,
learning elements of Protestantism and of a western life-style from
fellow Africans. He lived in a country ruled not by Europeans, but
by Afro-Americans, descendants of Africans who had been enslaved in the United States. Although they were from abroad, and
although they created a regime many native Liberians considered
oppressive, these Afro-American settlers demonstrated to the native
Liberians that people of African origin, like themselves, could have
a materially advanced standard of living and could rule their own
nation.

Harris's travels as a sailor had taken him to several African countries, including Nigeria, where there were both an educated African
elite and autonomous African Christian churches. Most of his own
religious experience in Liberia had been in a church where scriptures
and the church liturgy were in his own Grebo language. He was
also accustomed to a tradition of African Christian ministers and
evangelists who challenged the power of indigenous religious spirits
with that of the Christian god. Additionally, his educational level
had allowed him to hold several professional positions.

Harris's broad experience was unusual for a person of his place
and time. He had held positions of authority and importance and
had led people in sociopolitical activities that responded to his critical analysis of the existing social situation. As one who had lived in
different cultural settings, he was aware of some of the options
from which Africans, faced with some of the same basic problems
and presented with some of the same opportunities, could choose.
The modifications of religious and social life he proposed were

consistent with his own past experiences. The authority for his position, however, was seen by his converts, and by the prophet, as emanating not from Harris himself, but rather from the will of the Christian god.

Because he had experienced both traditional African and Western Christian life-styles, Harris's knowledge, attitude, and behavior were a synthesis of both. He was able to relate to and function in both worlds. He seems to have been able to talk on equal terms with Europeans, as well as with fellow Africans. His power was stronger than that of the traditional priests: he drove away the spirits they represented and did not hesitate to violate their taboos with no ill effects. He also pitted his power successfully against that of the Europeans, as is exemplified by the death of the colonial officer who mistreated him, the burning of the ship being unloaded on the Sabbath, and the prison door that persisted in opening of its own accord. Harris's role as a transitional figure with a foot in each society symbolized for his followers the ability of Africans to acquire modern expertise. His message and personal example conveyed to his converts both the spiritual and the practical techniques necessary for emulating him and for acquiring new knowledge and abilities.

The Prophet Harris inspired western-educated Africans, French colonial administrators, and some (mainly Protestant) missionaries to comment favorably about him. Joseph E. Casely Hayford, Gold Coast lawyer, politician, and writer, was impressed by Harris during the prophet's brief stay in his country. Hayford had written a book entitled *Ethiopia Unbound* (1911) in which he appealed to Africans to defend their indigenous institutions and cultures from colonial attack and to maintain their dignity as Africans. In 1911 he founded the Congress of British West Africa to help realize these goals (J. Harris 1972: 188). Hayford subsequently authored a book about Harris, entitled *William Waddy Harris: The West African Reformer—The Man and His Message*, in which he wrote:

> You cannot be in his presence for long without realising that you are in contact with a great personality. He began as a reformer in the state. He ended as a reformer in the spiritual realm. He is a dynamic force of a rare order. He will move this age as few have done. William Waddy Harris is a force to reckon with in the West

African experience in an age of doubt and hesitancy. [Hayford 1915: 5–7, 19]

Protestant missionary Pierre Benoit described the prophet as a "Man of Destiny." "As I listen to him," he said, "I feel that this man has caught something of the accents of the great prophets; their convictions, their uncompromising spirit, their divine enthusiasm are found again in him. Many have trembled before him; many have hated or adored him, and tens of thousands have feared him" (F. Walker 1927b: 109, 111).

Another Protestant missionary, Jean Bianquis, cited various sources that commented on Harris, including administrative reports, Catholic documents, and a manuscript written by an African Protestant. He concluded: "They all agree in representing Harris to us as a man gifted with a great power of persuasion, who exercised a profound influence and brought about a veritable religious revolution over a very vast territory" (1924: 1089). Catholic missionaries, on the other hand, characterized Harris as a "charlatan" and a "hypnotizer." Bianquis countered, however, that such descriptions conflicted with the positive evaluations of several colonial administrators and were not representative of the extent and depth of the moral and religious revolution that Harris was generally acknowledged to have produced almost single-handedly (1924: 1096).

The Prophet's Compatibility with Tradition

Harrists and non-Harrists alike concur that it was remarkable for a native Liberian to have had such a profound and revolutionary effect on so many people of diverse ethnic groups in the Ivory Coast in such a brief time, even creating a sense of unity among groups formerly antagonistic to one another. Precisely because Harris was not a native Ivorian, he was able to create a movement transcending ethnic particularisms. Not being a product of the same sociopolitical situation as his followers, he had an appeal that was not based on specific temporal issues. Although fitting a given historical moment, that appeal focused on general problems common to all members of his audience.

The area from which Harris came was also a factor in his effectiveness. Before his arrival, members of the lagoons ethnic groups had made long, yearly pilgrimages to Tabou and Cape Palmas in Kru country to worship the especially powerful spirits Beugré and Zri-Gnaba. Some of the stronger spirits they worshiped at home had also been brought from that area. Because the power of these Kru spirits had been stronger and more all-encompassing than that of most of the lagoons spirits, special credence was lent to the message of the Kru-man who exhorted people to worship a new god whose power, he said, was greater than that of the protecting spirits they had known.

The emphasis on Harris's role as an introducer of something new should not obscure the fact that both his technique and his message fit into what was already a well-established pattern among the lagoons ethnic groups. His audience did not perceive him as representing a radical departure from tradition, but rather understood him within the context of familiar experience.

Alexander Alland's analysis of the way in which western medical practitioners were accepted within the context of Abron culture in the Ivory Coast sheds some light on the way in which Harris was perceived. Alland says, writing of the images members of a host culture form of outsiders playing new and often ambiguous roles in the contact situation:

> No matter what kind of face an actor may wish to present to strangers, the image he projects will be determined in part by the preconceived notions of the audience. These notions will center around the role system of the host culture. When the new role has an analogue in the host culture, the image formed will be found in this analogue, and the actor will be pegged into a previous existing part. This can create considerable difficulties for agents of social change, but it also serves to preserve, at least for a time, the existing role system. These analogue roles must be analyzed in terms of structure, i.e., the network of social relationships within a society, and in terms of the cognitive map associated with behavior, affects, and beliefs imbedded in the role system. [1964: 714]

The worship of new spirits brought by traveling priests was not new. Before Harris came to the Ivory Coast there had been a history of priests bringing new spirits from different areas and training people in the worship of them. These new spirits were accepted, and their cults spread over large areas in direct proportion to their proven effectiveness. The priests usually wore white garments, trained a local priesthood, and taught new rituals to be performed at specific cult sites. Harris, by the content of his message and the nature of his presentation, fit very neatly into this preexisting pattern, infusing it with new meaning. He differed from his predecessors in his claim to have been sent by the only real god, the creator god whom people must worship to the exclusion of all other spiritual beings. Harris's success as a prophet grew as he demonstrated the power of his god, just as the traditional spirits had acquired influence over large areas as they proved their effectiveness.

An account of Harris's call to his mission that differs from the generally accepted version involving the Angel Gabriel reflects the closeness of the parallel that some of his converts saw between Harris and the traditional priests.[2] This account, furnished by a Gambian Protestant named Campbell who was in the Ivory Coast during Harris's stay, states that Harris was a "great fetisher." One day, as he was finishing his ceremony in the usual way, he heard a voice behind him. Looking around, he saw a man who said to him: "You must not believe in this stick and in these amulets that are before you, because as you well know, they have no power. Take this (he is given a large cane) and go here and there, from place to place, to preach about Christ. Tell your neighbors first to believe, to abandon the fetishes (rocks, wood, and amulets) which represent nothing more than the objects they are. A great power is upon you" (Bianquis 1924: 1158).

This explanation of the beginning of Harris's mission, which is consistent with the way many of his converts perceived him, portrays Harris in the role of a traditional priest, converted to believe in and to represent a power superior to that of the indigenous spirits. The prophet's own version likened his call to that of the biblical prophets, an idea which, although entirely logical within the context of his Protestant background, was nevertheless foreign to the experience and conceptual system of his converts.

Harris saw himself as the last prophet in terms of the biblical tradition within which he situated himself, and he actually became the last prophet in terms of the indigenous religious history of the people he converted. By discrediting the nature spirits and teaching the

Ivorians to worship the creator god in their place, the Prophet Harris effectively ended the tradition of the introduction of new nature spirits by indigenous priests. Even more significantly, he succeeded in becoming the only prophet to have permanently influenced the religious orientation of almost all of the peoples of the southern Ivory Coast.

Words, Behavior, Symbols:
Discontinuity, Continuity, and Creative Ambivalence

Whereas the French Catholic missionaries had not succeeded in interesting the Ivorians in Christianity, Harris not only made it relevant and interesting to them, he also made it imperative. Although the content of his verbal message was similar to that of the missionaries, his form of presenting it was entirely different. One Protestant missionary avowed, "The truth is that a native Christian, penetrated by the spirit of God, knows much better than Europeans—Catholic or Protestant—how to find the pathway to the souls of his brothers and to lead them to repentance and eternal life" (Bianquis 1924: 1154). The differences between the prophet's verbal and behavioral messages and those of the missionaries partially explain why the Ivorians accepted the Christian message from him, but not from the missionaries, and also account for the different directions in which his teachings inevitably led his converts.

The prophet's verbal message led some of his converts to learn to be Christian within context of the missionary churches, whereas his behavioral message led others to develop their own version of Christianity. He told his converts to set up their own churches where there were none. He did not, however, tell them to establish their own version of a Christian doctrine and ritual, but rather to wait for the missionaries who would come to teach them the Christian way.

When John Ahui and his party informed the prophet that the missionaries with Bibles had come, but that many Ivorians were not satisfied with their methods and were seeking other alternatives, Harris gave them his approval to continue independently. Considering Harris's Protestant background, there is no indication that he expected the Ivorians' Christianity to diverge from the missionary Christian model, except perhaps for specific modifications concerning the taking of money for sacraments and the practice of polygamy.

Because Harris's form of self-presentation corresponded to a role already familiar within the coastal societies, it is not surprising that many of his converts believed that he had come to present them with a new version of their own indigenous religion. Little in the prophet's behavior associated him with the European missionaries, and because of their limited exposure to missionaries, the Ivorians probably did not perceive either the similarity of the messages or the fact that the African prophet was telling them to worship the god the foreign missionaries worshiped.

It appears, in fact, that Harris indicated that he was the prophet of the creator god, whom the Ivorians had not worshiped since the mythical time when their ancestors had alienated him, rather than of a foreign god, as the missionaries' god was seen to be. Through the Prophet Harris, the creator was offering the Ivorians a second opportunity to learn to worship him correctly. The Protestant missionary de Billy reports that Harris said, "The great God who created heaven and earth; He whose name your ancestors worshiped before the diabolical fetishes rendered them blind and deaf; this God has sent me to announce to you that the time is come in which He wishes to deliver you from the power of the devil who ruins you, drives you crazy, and kills you" (1955: 7).

Whereas the missionaries spoke in abstract terms about the benefits of worshiping the Christian god and the consequences of not doing so, Harris provided immediate and concrete proof of his claims. Learning to worship the missionaries' god was a lengthy process during which people had no spiritual protection, which is why villages that had agreed to convert in the past, finding themselves defenseless, had returned to time-proven methods. Harris provided his converts with immediate protection by means of the rite of baptism. Whereas the missionaries demanded blind faith, Harris furnished undeniable proof of the power of his god.

Harris's god, although much greater in scope and power than the spirits he replaced, behaved in important respects like them. He expressed his pleasure and displeasure in the same ways they did, rewarding people with material prosperity, large families, and long life and punishing them with sickness, misfortune, and death. Both Harris, in the role of prophet, and the new god whose messenger he was fit familiar traditional expectations; that they did so facilitated their acceptance by the Ivorians.

Harris's ritual accoutrements were also understood in the light of the traditional mind-set. His white robe, although perhaps modeled along the lines of the costumes of the biblical prophets, undoubtedly appeared to most of the Ivorians, unfamiliar with biblical prophets,[3] much like the white garments worn by traditional priests such as the priests of the widely worshiped river spirit Tano. Harris also baptized people with water from the gourd bowl he carried, just as these indigenous priests had used water to purify and protect people.

The prophet's cane-cross was seen by many as a seat of spiritual power, and the giant crosses put at the entrance to villages by Catholic missionaries continue to be seen in this way. When people who were closely associated with or were priests of the indigenous spirits touched Harris's cane-cross, they began to tremble. Thus the cross was obviously the seat of a spirit more powerful than the one they served. To symbolize his mandate, Harris gave crosses to delegates who came to see him from distant villages. With the crosses, they believed, he passed on to them some of the power of his god to take home with them, just as the delegates who had once gone to Kru country to consult and to worship Beugré or Zri-Gnaba had returned with objects infused with some of their power.

Inasmuch as most of the people could not read, Harris's Bible acquired a special value in itself, independent of its contents. Harris touched the Bible to the heads of people who were possessed by evil spirits; they were immediately calmed, and thus his converts assumed it to be a repository of spiritual power emanating from God. They were anxious to acquire this powerful book that contained the will of the prophet's god; it was essential that one be present in each of their churches.

The gourd rattles that the prophet and his entourage used to provide rhythm for their songs acquired meanings beyond the purely musical because of the function of these rattles in their own societies. Such rattles had been used to summon the protective spirits whose praises people wanted to sing. Harrist church members say that the gourd rattles are essential to their worship because the prophet told them the rattles helped to carry the congregation's prayers and songs to God.

Harris's style of worship was a major factor in his appeal to the masses. He and his women followers played the gourd rattles and sang and danced as the Ivorians had done for their traditional spirits. When his converts asked how they should worship Harris's god, he told them to dance as they had for the indigenous spirits and to sing their own songs, adding the name "God." Thus, although Harris's message was new, it came attired in traditional trappings.

On the basis of his study of the Aladura church in Nigeria, J. D. Y. Peel posits that a structural prerequisite for the development of an African Christian church is a membership characterized by the absence of the social ties fundamental to indigenous societies. Most of the members of the churches he studied were, he said, urbanized, western-schooled young men seeking a new social environment and value system to replace the one they had left behind with their rural origins (Peel 1968: 7–8). Peel's formulation applies neither to the Harrist movement nor to the Harrist church. Neither the movement nor the church has been an urban phenomenon or has served as a refuge for deracinated migrants seeking new social bonds. On the contrary, both the movement and the church have been distinctly village phenomena, and the village social structures and cultural values continue to play a more important role in people's lives than does membership in any specific church.

When Harris succeeded in converting people in a village, he converted the entire village, or large sections of it, from the top down. Once he had defeated the traditional priests by proving their spirits ineffective, those priests, along with the chiefs and elders whose power had depended upon the defeated spirits, allowed Harris to baptize them. The rest of the villagers followed their leaders in being baptized into the new religion just as they had been in the old. The chiefs and elders continued as leaders supportive of and supported by the new religion.

Conversion in the context of the Harrist movement therefore did not involve a reaction to an absence of social norms and values. Because Harris's conversions occurred in groups representative of the social structure, the social order of the village was not disrupted. The new religion moved into the niche in the society that the old one had vacated, with essentially the same personnel.

The Harrist movement, furthermore, supported the indigenous social structure at a time when it was being shaken by external pressures. The chiefs, elders, and traditional priests acquired renewed power and authority by converting to the religion of the Prophet Harris. Rather than developing as a substitute for social institutions that were breaking down or losing their hold, the Harrist movement fitted into the existing social structure and helped to reinforce and perpetuate it.

The interaction between Harris's missionarylike verbal message and his familiar behavioral style, then, allowed his converts the flexibility to pursue different paths in their efforts to be faithful to him. His exhortation to begin worshiping the Christian god led people to the missionary churches, which taught a new religious and social orientation based on the European cultural values of the missionaries. His personal example, however, led them to form their own autonomous church based upon indigenous African values. Thus, whereas some of his verbal cues led to a break with traditional religious behavior, his own behavior led to the legitimization of many elements of indigenous religious beliefs and practices, which became institutionalized by those people who became Harrist Christians.

Harris's influence allowed for conceptual as well as behavioral continuity between the traditional religious orientation and the new one he offered. It was the act of baptism that demarcated the transition from the old to the new practices. A person could accept Harris's baptism only if he or she agreed to renounce all indigenous religious practices. Baptism provided purification from previous sinful behavior as well as protection against future harm. People could not revert to their old habits after being baptized because they would incur God's wrath and punishment; the act of baptism closed the door on one religious orientation and opened the door to a new one.

Although in a sense marking the moment of religious discontinuity, Harris's baptism could also be understood within the traditional conceptual framework. Washing ceremonies had been used in the past to purify people from previous sins and to protect them from future harm. Contrary to the European missionaries, Harris insisted that baptism must mark the first stage of conversion. As an act of initiation into the cult of the new deity, the rite of baptism provided immediate replacement for the sources of spiritual protection of the past.

In view of such evident social and conceptual continuity, one must seriously question the missionary contention that Harris created a "clean break" with the indigenous religion, morally and psychologically transforming his converts. One Protestant missionary reported that as a result of Harris's effect, people had forsaken their traditional religion, so that the "outward institutions and tokens of fetishism were swept clean away. It was as if some fierce fire had passed through the dense bush of tribal superstition and consumed everything in its path" (Thompson 1928: 633). Indeed, fierce fires had destroyed just what the missionary said they had—outward tokens.

Harris did not destroy the traditional religious system, creating a clean break with the past and clearing the way for totally new religious behavior, as the missionaries maintained. Rather than completely giving up their indigenous religious concepts in exchange for the frequently inappropriate concepts of European Christianity, as many missionaries expected, the Ivorians understood the new in terms of the old. Christianity did not replace the indigenous religion. It was instead interpreted according to indigenous categories and meanings, which it, in turn, modified in the process.

Because some fundamental indigenous beliefs and practices had been discredited by Harris, his converts were obliged to create replacements or modifications. Harris provided both the inspiration and the resources for doing so. His version of Christianity provided new organizational and conceptual tools that the Ivorians could use to cope with the perennial problems internal to their own societies, as well as with new problems of exogenous origin.

Because of the composite nature of Harris's appeal, based as it was on a synthesis of elements from the various aspects of his own experience, he was perceived in a variety of ways. He saw himself in the role of a biblical prophet. Even though he was generous enough to send them his converts, the Catholic missionaries viewed him as a charlatan and a victim of delusions, who, fortunately for them, had a greater appeal for the Africans than they could hope to attain. The Protestants saw him as a divine messenger, sent by God to play the role of John the Baptist, paving the way for their own arrival. Each perception of him was commensurate with the background, experiences, world view, and self-interest of those who so characterized him.

His African followers saw him as functioning in the role of their traditional priests, but as representing a more powerful deity. Whereas outside observers thought that he was creating a clean break with the past, the Ivorians saw their conversion experience as a variation on a continuing theme. His converts regarded the prophet as bringing them not a new religion, but rather a stronger, more effective, version of the old, and even an opportunity to return to that religion's original and most perfect form.

Because of his charismatic power and the liberating nature of his mission, Harris had many potential enemies—the traditional priests whose power he challenged; the chiefs whose power was sustained by these priests; the colonial administrators who were apprehensive of any mass action directed by African initiative; and the missionaries, whose Christianizing task he accomplished much better than they did and who thus might have seen in his procedures a serious critique of their methods.

Nevertheless, the extraordinary prophet managed to please and impress the majority of the people he encountered and to win the approval of very diverse groups. The French tolerated him because he did not engage in direct political action and because he encouraged the Ivorians to work hard and to cooperate more fully with the administration. The missionaries were pleased with him because he sent them the converts that their own methods could not attract. The traditional chiefs and priests were pleased because they continued to occupy important positions in the new religion, just as in the old. The people he converted were pleased because he had brought them a god who was more powerful, more concerned with their daily affairs, and less abusive than the traditional spirits had been, and one whom they could worship in a familiar way.

Harris provided both a prototype for a Christianity that could be adapted to an African life-style and also a way in which an African religious system could be modified to fit the Christian framework with little injustice to either. He told the Africans to adjust to and model themselves after the Europeans in educational goals and technological knowledge. He demonstrated to them how they could accomplish these beneficial changes in ways that would not shake their own world view.

A Prophet of Liberation

Because of his own historical experiences, Harris's preaching of the Word of God was of necessity based on premises very different from those of the missionaries, and directed toward fundamentally different ends. It is important to keep in mind that European Christian missionaries in Africa functioned for the most part as direct agents of colonialism. Indeed, the Catholic missionaries were summoned to the Ivory Coast by the colonial administration to inculcate loyalty to France in their Ivorian subjects. Their Christianity was to be used to indoctrinate the Africans into accepting their oppressed status docilely. They were a part of the apparatus intended to transform the recently colonized Africans from their previous status of sovereignty and equality to that of willing subjects of their new colonial masters, henceforth to labor for the benefit of France.

The missionaries' goal, then, was not just to convert Africans to Christianity, but also to use the church to resocialize and control them. This aim was especially evident in the collusion of the Catholic missionaries and the colonial officials in persecuting the Harrist Protestants who tried to be autonomous Christians. Harrists say that after Benoit's visit to the prophet in Liberia, the Protestants told them that he was dead. In order to present themselves as the only legitimate heirs to the prophet's work, the missionaries attempted to deprive the Ivorians of the reinforcement they needed in order to create an autonomous Christian institution.

It is also apparent that the Europeans did not have a very high opinion of the people they so easily and unself-consciously referred to as "savages." Harris, being a member of that large portion of humankind collectively referred to by those of Eurocentric bent as "savage," clearly saw Christianity as playing a very different kind of role vis-à-vis the Africans. Rather than offering the Ivorians a message of Christianity in the service of their oppression, as the missionaries had done, he offered them a message of liberation. He wanted to free them from the narrow constraints of the indigenous religions, as well as from European domination.

Christianity had been introduced into Liberia and other parts of Africa to "civilize the heathens." At least from the Christian perspective, Harris was living proof of the success of that endeavor. His accomplishments in Liberia—his career positions and material lifestyle—were sufficient indications of the value of Christianization and the attendant educational process. He spent most of his life as preacher and teacher, sharing the benefits of his exposure with his Liberian compatriots. Born of non-Christian parents, Harris had nevertheless come to direct a school and even to challenge the Liberian government.

As an independent nation, Liberia had goals different from those of the colonial government of the Ivory Coast. The Afro-Americans who settled in Liberia had left behind an oppressive racial situation in the United States, and many believed that they would find freedom in Africa. Their leaders expected to bring the benefits of their life-style to the Africans, to serve as examples and work for the redemption of all people of African origin. Although they set up an imperfect system, allowing many of the social inequities of which they themselves had been victims to persist, many of them had returned to Africa in full awareness of their kinship with the indigenous Africans.

The goal of the European colonizers was entirely different. The sole purpose for the establishment of the Ivorian colony was to enrich France, the country that first succeeded in staking a claim to the territory during the nineteenth-century European "scramble for Africa." The function the Africans were required to fulfill was the same as that of their kin who had been enslaved and taken to the Americas—they were to work not for their own prosperity, but for that of the whites who had by armed force gained control over them. The European colonists clearly felt no sense of human kinship with the people whom they considered savages and whom they so freely brutalized. Thus, both Christianity and the mission education that accompanied it were designed to train the Africans to occupy their proper "place"—at the bottom of the colonial hierarchy. The Europeans did not intend to train the Africans, as the Afro-Americans in Liberia did, to become integrated into the total social network.

Because he exhibited in his message and example the influence of Pan-Africanist Afro-American leaders like Blyden, Harris's impact was, in a colonial setting, revolutionary. Consequently, Harris was expelled from two colonies by two different colonial powers, in spite of what both acknowledged as his positive effects on the indigenous people. Whereas the French saw Harris as introducing a Protestant and hence rival British influence among the Ivorians, the British Gold Coast colonial administrators also hastened to invite him to leave their territory. Although he accomplished the kinds of behavioral changes in the African populations that the colonialists had been unsuccessful in attaining, both the English and the French subordinated their desire to attain such results to their desire to keep their subjects under control.

Neither colonial power was willing to tolerate the particular Christian message of the phenomenal Liberian prophet. Neither was willing to permit its subjects too much exposure to the model he represented—that of a staunchly independent African determined to spread his message internationally and able to interact on equal footing with European colonial officials and missionaries. Believing himself to be directly mandated by God to bring this message to the Africans, Harris was able to mobilize and influence multitudes of people. As an African with the knowledge and skills of the west, which he had acquired from repatriated Afro-American freedom seekers in Liberia, Harris served as a symbol for the Ivorians of their own potentiality and became one of the best known and most influential prophets in African religious history.

His basic spiritual message was similar to the one he had preached as a lay evangelist in Liberia and also to the one the foreign missionaries preached: the Africans should acknowledge the superiority of the Christian god to the indigenous spirits, and should hasten to worship him. Had he limited himself to such common evangelizing, however, he would have had no greater impact and acquired no greater renown than did the thousands of other anonymous evangelists and missionaries of turn-of-the-century West Africa. His unprecedented and profound impact resulted because there was something more to his message than the common exhortation to worship the Christian god. He was not like the traditional Christian evangelizers who promised only hope in a remote and nebulous afterlife. Harris offered the pragmatic promise of an improved life on earth and provided immediate and tangible evidence of the power of his beliefs.

It was this difference that made Joseph E. Casely Hayford's 1915 statement so true. The Prophet Harris did indeed "move the religious life of the area he touched as no one before or after has done," and he was "a force for both Africans and colonial Europeans to reckon with" (pp. 6–7, 19). The Europeans initially praised and then persecuted him. The Africans tested him and then followed him and allowed him to change their lives radically. He provided direction—several possible directions, in fact—for African self-realization in that tumultuous period. The people who joined the missionary churches, as well as those who created their own institutions, did so expressly on the basis of Harris's divine authority.

Harris offered to the Ivorians the tools of both spiritual and secular autonomy. On the spiritual level, his message was that the Ivorians were putting their faith in minor spiritual entities when they should be worshiping the universal creator god, who was rightfully angered by his creatures' failure to worship him. Rather than working constructively toward their own prosperity with the help of their creator, they preyed on each other through witchcraft. It was not surprising, therefore, that they had been conquered by people who, in spite of the very un-Christian oppression they unleashed on the African people, did worship the Christian god. The universal god had finally sent the Africans their own prophet in the person of William Wade Harris to show them the path of salvation.

Harris's secular message enlightened the Ivorians about the pragmatic steps to take, beyond correct prayer and worship, to actualize his program for liberation. If they worked diligently and sought to become educated, he told them, in seven years they could be on the same level as the Europeans. He was himself the product of such a process. As the result of fewer than seven years of schooling in an era when fewer years of schooling were required of everyone, he had acquired the background that prepared him for the various leadership roles that he had fulfilled.

Thus, Harris's message countered the definition of the relationship between Africans and Europeans contained in the foreign missionaries' brand of Christianity. He told and showed the Africans that they could be equal to the Europeans, not subordinate, thereby providing a radical message of reassurance to recently defeated but once sovereign people.

Harris had told his Ivorian converts that Catholic and Protestant missionaries would teach them Christianity. From his own experience in Liberia, where the Protestants had provided him with the teaching that allowed him to believe that he was God's last prophet, he had little reason to suspect the motives of the European missionaries. He could not have known that the missionary schools in the Ivory Coast would train Africans to fill the low-level needs of the colonial enterprise, but not to direct African schools or to govern their own country. In Liberia, Afro-American and Euro-American missionaries had readied Africans like himself to take greater control over their own destinies and had equipped African leaders to teach other Africans to do so. Harris's experience could not have prepared him, either, for the Catholic collusion in seeking to destroy his movement. Knowledge of these facts, in conjunction with his own frustration at being prohibited by the French from continuing his urgent task, led Harris to readjust his perspective on the Europeans and their missionaries. As a result of colonial violence against him, the prophet said to the delegation from Petit Bassam what the French had always feared he would say to the multitudes in Ivory Coast—that France would suffer because of its oppression of Africans and that the Ivorians should refuse to assist further in the French imperial scheme that had already deprived them of their sovereignty.

Because Harris and his followers had experienced oppression, it was reasonable for him to tell the Ivorian delegation not to let the Europeans take further advantage of them, but to insist upon forging their own path independently. If they were to be Christians inspired by the prophet's message of liberation, they had no choice but to create their own institution. Thus, the Harrist church is the living symbol of one group of Ivorians' uncompromising insistence upon being not the kinds of colonized Christians the missionaries wanted them to become, but the kinds of independent African Christians epitomized by the example of the Prophet Harris.

The Harrist church provides proof of the adequacy and viability of indigenous African social and conceptual structures in adapting to the changed demands of the new reality. They form the basis of the African church that has taken its place alongside Islam, Protestantism, and Catholicism as a national religion in the Ivory Coast. The Harrist church was created by and for people who wanted to be Christian, who preferred their own world view and their own social system to any imported variety, and who insisted upon making modifications in the latter according to their own criteria and interests.

The Harrist church thus represents a dual critique of aspects of the indigenous system and of missionary Christianity. The indigenous religion, based on the village life-styles of which it was a part, was inadequate to explain the much more diverse and complex human interactions created by colonialism. And missionary Christianity was oriented toward imposing radical change in the African societies to force them to conform to European tastes and interests. Harris had told his converts that they must become Christian or face certain destruction. The Prophet Harris, whom Harrist songs praise as "the bringer of a message that would liberate us," did liberate his converts from both the constraints of the indigenous system and those of colonial Christianity, allowing them to create their own African synthesis. The Harrist church, the institutionalization of the amazing prophet's unique Christian message, remains a living symbol of African integrity and determination and of the inevitable triumph of indigenous initiative in determining the future of the African continent.

Notes

Introduction

1. See S. Walker (1979*a*) for a description and analysis of other Harrist churches: Crastchotche; the Deima church; the Church of the Twelve Apostles in Ghana; and the churches of Bodjo Aké, Jonas Zaka, Bébéh Gra, and Papa Nouveau.

2. Parrinder said that of a total of 68 million Christians, 22 million were Protestant, 30 million were Catholic, about 8 million were Coptic or Orthodox, and over 7 million were members of the various African Christian churches (1969: 167).

3. See, for example, Baëta (1962); Ayandele (1970); Peel (1968); Turner (1966*a*); and Webster (1964).

4. 1968: 20. Although acknowledging its atypical origin as an expression of African initiative, Barrett nonetheless suggests that the Harrist movement should be classified with the movements of separation from the missionary churches (p. 53). He bases this contention on the erroneous statement that the Harrist movement took root in a milieu characterized by decades of missionary contact, in which there was a sizable Christianized community. Indeed, the first Catholic missionary effort in the Ivory Coast occurred in the 1600s, but the missionaries had been totally unsuccessful in establishing a lasting influence, and had not been located in the area where the Harrist movement took root.

Chapter One

1. Although Blyden was an influential thinker and leader in Liberia, as might be expected, the majority of Afro-American settlers nonetheless believed that they possessed a superior life-style, worthy of emulation by the Africans. Shick makes the point, however, that although many Afro-Americans expected the Africans to give up their own culture and traditions in order to take on the benefits of "Civilization and Christianity," the realities of their own need to adapt to the new environment required

them to make many compromises with indigenous practices (1977: 60–61).

2. See Haliburton (1971) for a more extensive historical view of Harris's background and activities.

3. Haliburton 1971: 11–14. Interestingly, the Reverend S. W. Kla Seton is reported to have left the Episcopal church and to have presided from 1887 to 1897 over a Russellite or Jehovah's Witness church, in which he said that he preached the "pure Word of God," and in which polygamy was allowed (Haliburton 1971: 15).

4. Finding the Christianity of the Bible more acceptable than its Europeanized interpretation by the missionaries, many African Christian churches incorporated biblically justified polygamy into their doctrines. Barrett notes that the European Christian attitude toward polygamy was a matter of dispute even during the Middle Ages. Saint Augustine maintained that polygamy was justified only for the multiplication of the human race. Calvin, however, proscribed it and condemned the biblical patriarchs who practiced it. Luther said that although monogamy was obligatory, whatever was permitted by the law of Moses was still permissible. He advised against polygamy, but at one time acknowledged that according to the Gospel, a Christian could have more than one wife. The Council of Trent anathematized this permissive view toward polygamy, and the question was settled until Christianity spread out of Europe. Then the missionaries maintained that polygamy was incompatible with the teachings of Christianity (Barrett 1968: 116–17).

5. Different accounts attribute different ages to the prophet. It is sure only that he was quite aged, but very sturdy, during his travels along the coast to pursue his mission.

6. In a rather fanciful account of the prophet's life, Musson says that he added "William Harris" in recognition of a kindly ship captain by that name for whom he worked (1950: 52).

7. Members of the Kru language family were known along the West African coast as hard workers. They were frequently praised for their good work as "crewmen" (or "crewboys") on the European merchant vessels that traveled along the coast. Hence the equivalence of "Kruman" and "crewman."

8. The accused person was forced to drink a potion made from sasswood bark. If the person was innocent, he or she was expected to experience no ill effects, but if guilty, the person was expected to die.

9. The authors who described Harris as a curious folkloric figure were unaware of his background, only recently researched by Haliburton (1971), and knew only of his career as a prophet. These writers were also European missionaries or colonial officials who shared a biased and eth-

nocentric conception of Africans, one that was usually not open to influence from the objective realities that challenged it.

10. Platt 1934: 52–53. Most of Benoit's report of his visit to the prophet is reproduced in this source.

11. Alexander Crummell had also been influential in Maryland County, although before William Wade Harris's time (*Newsletter* 1980: 7–8).

Chapter Two

1. There is little record of Harris's activities in the Kru-speaking area that lies between the Liberian border and the lagoons region of the Ivory Coast, and no indication that he had much influence there.

2. The names of ethnic groups are spelled according to French phonetics because that is how they appear in most of the literature on the area.

3. Although the Ebrié acknowledge the continued existence of the nature spirits, the Christianity of the Prophet Harris superseded their concern with these lesser spiritual forces, and some spirits are said to have fled in acknowledgment of the stronger force of Harris's god.

4. This is the same gesture, interestingly, that Harris made in protesting against the Liberian government.

Chapter Three

1. Actually, late 1913.

2. The term "fetish" has been used by Europeans and Americans to designate in a derogatory manner the material objects in which Africans believe spiritual beings can reside, and which consequently are loci of spiritual power. "Fetisher" thus is the term used for an indigenous priest, and "fetishism" indicates an indigenous religious system. The Ivorians learned these terms from the French colonizers. They are used disdainfully by the Ivorians who have become Harrists, Protestants, or Catholics, just as they are by the French. For those Ivorians who continue their traditional beliefs and practices, however, the terms have no negative connotations. Many Africans have been quick to perceive the similarities between their own "fetishes" and the crosses, statues of saints, and other artifacts of Christianity that were brought to Africa by the European missionaries.

3. The river separating the Ivory Coast and Liberia is Cavally in French, Cavalla in English.

4. Armstrong 1920: 39–40. In fact, an Nzima woman, Grace Thannie, went back with him to the Ivory Coast. Later she returned to the Gold Coast to found a church inspired by Harris, which she called the Church of the Twelve Apostles. Cf. S. Walker (1979*b*).

Chapter Four

1. Bianquis specifies Sierra Leone perhaps because the Protestant missionaries in the Ivory Coast heard about Harris when he was evangelizing in Sierra Leone. It is also possible that Bianquis took the prophet to be a native of Sierra Leone because many of his clerk-disciples were.

2. It is quite probable that this statement is a biblical reference in which Ethiopia refers to the continent of Africa. Harris was thus perhaps making a political reference to the colonial situation in the Ivory Coast and most of the rest of Africa, now that he had suffered at the hands of the European colonizers. This was just the kind of advice from the prophet to his followers—not to serve the interests of the European colonizers—that the French administration had feared when they expelled him in 1914. Some Harrists see this reference as a forecast of Italy's subsequent invasion of Ethiopia, and therefore as evidence of Harris's great psychic powers.

3. Incomplete reference to a biblical passage.

4. Perhaps a reference to the final defeat of the Grebo by the Liberian government.

5. Isa. 4:1 reads: "And in that day seven women shall take hold of one man, saying we will eat our own bread, and wear our own apparel; only let us be called by thy name, to take away our reproach." This seems to be the relevant verse: it refers to and condones polygamy, one of the issues of concern to the Ivorian delegation.

6. Mark 10:2–12 also discusses the institution of marriage:

And the Pharisees came to him, and asked him, Is it lawful for a man to put away his wife: tempting him. And he answered and said unto them, What did Moses command you? And they said, Moses suffered to write a bill of divorcement, and to put her away. And Jesus answered and said unto them, For the hardness of your heart he wrote you this precept. But from the beginning of the creation God made them male and female. For this cause shall a man leave his father and mother, and cleave to his wife; And they twain shall be one flesh; so then they are no more twain, but one flesh. What therefore God hath joined together, let no man put asunder. And in the house his disciples asked him again of the same matter. And he saith unto them, Whosoever shall put away his wife, and marry another, committeth adultery against her. And if a woman shall put away her husband and be married to another, she committeth adultery.

7. This is probably Dougbo.

8. In a footnote, Amos-Djoro notes that it is strange that Harris used an X instead of signing his name, because he was literate and had signed his name on the message he had given to Benoit (1956: 225). It is possible that the prophet was unable to sign his name at this time because of his advanced age.

9. Chief Nandjui.

10. The Prophet Harris died the year following the visit of the Ivorian delegation.

Chapter Six

1. The androcentric social structure has not yet imagined the possibility of giving such important public roles to women. For information on the role of women in various Harris-inspired religious institutions, see S. Walker (1979a).

2. Parrinder notes that most African Christian churches permit polygamy among the members, but not among the clergy, a practice consistent with the New Testament writings of the apostle Paul in 1 Tim. 3:2, 12 (1969: 150).

3. For a discussion of some of the issues involved in creating this allegiance, see S. Walker (1980a: 134; 1979b: 25).

4. For further discussion of the relationship between young men and their elders, see S. Walker (1980b).

5. Fortunately, I was able to attend this conference.

6. In this developing country in which only a small portion of the total population is literate, the meaning of the term "intellectual" may be stretched to include anyone with some secondary school education.

7. For a greater understanding of Atcho's role in the Harrist church, see S. Walker (1980a); Augé et al (1975); and Rouch (1963).

Chapter Seven

1. In the 1955 Census of the Commune of Abidjan, the Harrists were listed as constituting 2 percent of the Christians (who as a group consti-

tuted 43 percent of the total) in the population, numbering 2,222 members out of 111,925 inhabitants. The Harrists constituted an important proportion of the Ebrié, with 20.8 percent, and of the Alladian, with 11.4 percent. These two groups are the most highly Christianized in the country, being 99.2 and 97.7 percent Christian respectively. Among the other lagoons ethnic groups, the Harrists constituted 5.1 percent of the Attié and 0.3 percent of the Adjoukrou (Recensement d'Abidjan 1955: 29, 32). These numbers were by no means representative of the total Harrist population, because most Harrists lived in villages, not in the capital.

2. A date irrelevant to Harrist history because the Prophet Harris did not arrive in the Ivory Coast until 1913.

3. See n. 7 to Chapter 6.

Chapter Eight

1. Of course, the idea of witchcraft is not peculiar to the Ivorians, or to Africa. People said to be witches were burned at the stake in both Europe and the United States. The Ivorians do not, however, kill their suspected witches. Such punishment is left to God.

2. This change in the locus of responsibility for evil is the most basic commonality among all the religious groups that developed as a result of Harris's influence. (See S. Walker 1979a.)

3. The pre-Harrist idea that some people have "a stronger spirit" than others, which explains their success, has not entirely disappeared, but it is not congruent with the formal doctrine.

4. See S. Walker (1980b) for further discussion of this issue.

Chapter Nine

1. S. Walker (1979a) discusses the relationship between Harris's style of presentation and the different ways in which his verbal and behavioral messages were implemented by religious groups inspired by him in the Ivory Coast and Ghana.

2. There is another account of the origin of his call offered by an anonymous author in a Protestant missionary journal and not mentioned elsewhere. According to this version, Harris was walking in the forest one day when he suddenly found himself face to face with a leopard. Unarmed, and fearing for his life, he prayed to God, promising that if he were saved he would spend the rest of his life serving the Lord. The leop-

ard turned away and Harris set out to fulfill his pledge ("Thirty Thousand Christians" 1924: 59). This version is probably most useful as an indication of the kinds of myths that grew up around the man who influenced many lives in different kinds of ways.

3. They were equally unfamiliar with Hausa traders and foreign missionaries, whose garments may have been models for Harris's. There were very few of either in the Ivorian environment.

References

Ajayi, J. F. Ade, and Ayandele, A. E. 1969. Writing African Church History. In *The Church Crossing Frontiers*, eds. Peter Beyerhaus and Carl F. Hallencreutz. Uppsala: Gleerup.

Akré Loba, Absalom. 1969–70. Harrisme et fétichisme en basse Côte d'Ivoire. Final examination, Athenée Royale d'Ixelles, Brussels.

Alland, Alexander, Jr. 1964. Native Therapists and Western Medical Practitioners among the Abron of Ivory Coast. *Transactions of the New York Academy of Sciences* 26(6): 714–25.

Amon d'Aby, J. F. 1951. *La Côte d'Ivoire dans la cité africaine*. Paris: Editions Larose.

Amos-Djoro, Ernest. 1966. Les Eglises Harristes et le nationalisme ivoirien. *Le Mois en Afrique* 5: 26–47.

———. 1956. Prophétisme et nationalisme africains: les Harristes en Côte d'Ivoire. Ph.D. dissertation, Ecole Pratique des Hautes Etudes, Section des Sciences Religieuses, Paris.

Angoulvant, Gabriel. 1916. *La Pacification de la Côte d'Ivoire, 1908–1916: méthodes et résultats*. Paris: Emile Lacrose, Libraire-Editeur.

Annuaire nationale de la Côte d'Ivoire. 1966. Abidjan: Ministère de l'Information.

Armstrong, Charles W. 1920. *The Winning of West Africa*. London: Wesleyan Methodist Missionary Society.

Augé, Marc. 1969. *Le Rivage alladian: Organisation et évolution des villages alladian*. Paris: Office de la Recherche Scientifique et Technique d'Outre-Mer (ORSTOM).

———, et al. 1975. *Prophétisme et thérapeutique: Albert Atcho et la communauté de Bregbo*. Paris: Hermann.

Ayandele, E. A. 1970. *Holy Johnson: Pioneer of African Nationalism*. New York: Humanities Press.

Babi, René. 1969a. L'Eglise Harriste de Côte d'Ivoire: Les Continuateurs de W. W. Harris. *Eburnéa* 29 (October): 16–20.

———. 1969b. L'Eglise Harriste de Côte d'Ivoire: Naissance et expansion. *Eburnéa* 28 (September): 2–7.

Baëta, C. G. 1962. *Prophetism in Ghana: A Study of Some "Spiritual"*

Churches. London: Student Christian Movement Press.

Balandier, Georges. 1963. *Sociologie actuelle de L'Afrique noire*. Paris: Presses Universitaires de France.

Barber, Bernard. 1914. Acculturation and Messianic Movements. *American Sociological Review* 6: 663–69.

Barrett, David B. 1968. *Schism and Renewal in Africa: An Analysis of Six Thousand Contemporary Religious Movements*. Nairobi: Oxford University Press.

Bartels, Francis L. 1965. *The Roots of Ghana Methodism*. Cambridge: Cambridge University Press.

Bastide, R. 1961. Messianismes et développement économique et social. *Cahiers Internationaux de Sociologie* 31: 3–14.

———. 1956. "La Causalité externe et la causalité interne dans l'explication sociologique. *Cahiers Internationaux de Sociologie* 21: 77–79.

Bernus, Edmond. 1957. Ahouati: Notes sur un village dida. *Etudes Eburnéenes* 6: 213–29.

Bianquis, Jean. 1924. "Dix ans d'histoire religieuse à la Côte d'Ivoire." *Foi et Vie* 1 (16 November): 1086–1106; 2 (1 December): 1144–58.

Blyden, Edward W. 1908. *African Life and Customs*. London: C. M. Phillips Co.

———. 1887. *Christianity, Islam, and the Negro Race*. London: W. B. Whittingham and Co. Reprint. Edinburgh, Edinburgh University Press, 1967.

Bond, George; Johnson, Walton; and Walker, Sheila S., eds. 1979. *African Christianity: Patterns of Religious Continuity*. New York: Academic Press.

Bonnefoy, C. 1954. Tiagba: Notes sur un village aizi. *Etudes Eburnéenes* 3: 7–129.

Boudet, L. 1910. Autrefois chez les Attiés. *Journal Officiel de la Côte d'Ivoire* (13 January). Reprinted in *Eburnéa* 21 (1 January 1969): 12–16.

Boulnois, J. 1933. *Gnon-Sua: Dieu des Guérés*. Paris: L. Fournier.

Bouscayrol, R. 1949. Notes sur le peuple ebrié. *Bulletin de l'Institut Fondamental d'Afrique Noire* 11(3–4): 383–408.

Bureau, René. 1971. Le Prophète Harris et la religion Harriste. Institut d'Ethnosociologie, Université d'Abidjan, Ivory Coast.

———. n.d.*a*. L'Eglise Harriste: Bregbo. Unpublished manuscript.

———. n.d.*b*. William Wade Harris et le Harrisme: Côte d'Ivoire, 1913–1966. Unpublished manuscript.

Burridge, Kenelm. 1969. *New Heaven, New Earth*. Oxford: Basil Clackwell.

———. 1960. *Mambu: A Melanesian Millennium*. London: Methuen and Co.

Campbell, Penelope. 1971. *Maryland in Africa: The Maryland State Colonization Society, 1831–1857*. Urbana: University of Illinois Press.

Carey, Lott. 1837/1971. Letters. Reprinted in *Apropos of Africa: Afro-American Leaders and the Romance of Africa*, eds. Adelaide Cromwell Hill and Martin Kilson, pp. 90–97. Garden City, N.Y.: Doubleday and Co.

Cason, John W. 1962. The Growth of Christianity in the Liberian Environment. Ph.D. dissertation, Columbia University, New York.

Ching, Donald S. 1950. *Ivory Tales*. London: Epworth Press.

Clignet, Rémi, and Foster, Philip. 1966. *The Fortunate Few: A Study of Secondary Schools and Students in the Ivory Coast*. Evanston, Ill.: Northwestern University Press.

Cooksey, J. J., and McLeish, A. 1931. *Religion and Civilization in West Africa*. London: World Dominion Press.

Côte d'Ivoire: Encyclopédie Africaine et Malgache. 1964. Paris: Larousse.

Crummell, Alexander. 1891. *Africa and America*. Springfield, Mass.: Willey and Co.

———. 1862. *The Future of Africa: Being Addresses, Sermons, etc., Delivered in the Republic of Liberia*. New York: Charles Scribner's Sons.

———. 1861/1971. The Relations and Duties of Free Colored Men in America to Africa. Reprinted in *Apropos of Africa: Afro-American Leaders and the Romance of Africa*, eds. Adelaide Cromwell Hill and Martin Kilson, pp. 98–107. Garden City, N.Y.: Doubleday and Co.

de Billy, Pasteur E. 1955. Le Prophète Harris en Côte d'Ivoire. *Envol* (March): 7–20.

Désanti, Dominique. 1962. *Côte d'Ivoire*. Lausanne: L'Atlas des Voyages Rencontres.

Dieterlen, Germaine, ed. 1965. *Textes sacrés de l'Afrique noire*. Paris: Gallimard.

Dupire, Marguerite. 1960. Planteurs autochtones et étrangers en Basse-Côte d'Ivoire orientale. *Etudes Eburnéenes* 8: 7–237.

———, and Boutillier, Jean-Louis. 1958. Le Pays adioukrou et sa palmeraie. *L'Homme d'Outre Mer* 4. Paris: Office de la Recherche Scientifique et Technique d'Outre-Mer (ORSTOM).

Egny, Pégard. 1972. L'Eglise Harriste veut s'adapter aux réalitiés du XXième siecle. *Fraternité Matin* (Abidjan), 5 September.

Enquête Démographique, Résultats Définitifs, République Togolaise, vol. 11. 1961. Ministère des Finances, de l'Economie et du Plan, Service de la Statistique Générale.

Fasholé-Luke, George, et al., eds. 1978. *Christianity in Independent Africa*. London: Rex Corlingas.

Fernandez, James W. 1979. Introduction to *The New Religions of Africa*, ed. Bennetta Jules-Rosette, pp. xvii–xix. Norwood, N.J.: Ablex Publishing Corp.

————. 1969. *Microcosmogony and Modernization in African Religious Movements*. Occasional Paper Series, No. 3, Centre of Developing Studies. Montreal: McGill University.

————. 1964. African Religious Movements: Types and Dynamics. *Journal of Modern African Studies* 2(4): 531–49.

Gibson, Stephen J. 1920. How the Gates Are Lifted on the Gold Coast. *Foreign Field*, January, pp. 59–60.

Gorju, Joseph. 1917. La Côte d'Ivoire chrétienne pendant la guerre. *Missions Catholiques* 49: 2531.

————. 1915. *La Côte d'Ivoire chrétienne*. Lyon: Librairie Catholique Emmanuel Vitte.

Grivot, R. 1942. Le Cercle de Lahou (Côte d'Ivoire). *Bulletin de l'Institut Fondamental d'Afrique Noire* 4(1–4): 1–154.

Gwaltney, John Langston. 1980. *Drylongso: A Self-Portrait of Black America*. New York: Random House.

Haliburton, Gordon Mackay. 1971. *The Prophet Harris*. London: Longman Group.

Harris, Joseph E. 1972. *Africans and Their History*. New York: New American Library.

Harris, Sheldon. 1972. *Paul Cuffee, Black America, and the African Return*. New York: Simon and Schuster.

Hayford, Joseph E. Casely. 1915. *William Waddy Harris: The West African Reformer—The Man and His Message*. London: C. M. Phillips.

————. 1911. *Ethiopia Unbound*. London: C. M. Phillips.

Hill, Adelaide Cromwell, and Kilson, Martin, eds. 1971. *Apropos of Africa: Afro-American Leaders and the Romance of Africa*. Garden City, N.Y.: Doubleday and Co.

Holas, B. 1969. Les Dieux d'Afrique noire. *Eburnéa* 21: 6–11.

————. 1965. *Le Séparatisme religieux en Afrique Noire: L'Example de la Côte d'Ivoire*. Paris: Presses Universitaires de France.

————. 1954. Bref aperçu sur les principaux cultes syncrétiques de la basse Côte d'Ivoire. *Africa* 24(1): 55–60.

Horler, Edmund C. 1918. Stretching Out Her Hands to God. *Foreign Field*, July, pp. 153–54.

Horton, Robin. 1971. African Conversion. *Africa* 61(2): 85–108.

Hultkrantz, Ake. 1969. Pagan and Christian Elements in the Religious Syncretism among the Shoshoni Indians of Wyoming. In *Syncretism*, ed. Sven S. Hartman, pp. 15–40. Stockholm: Almquist and Wicksell.

Ivory Coast, National Archives, Repository Collections. Rapport

Politique, 1951, Gouvernement Général de l'A.O.F., Territoire de la Côte d'Ivoire.

_____. Coutumes: Tribu Ebrié. 1933. Le Cercle des Lagunes, Abidjan, Colonie de la Côte d'Ivoire (28 June).

_____. Nouvelle religion venue de la côte. Extrait du Rapport Politique du 2e trimestre 1920, de la Subdivision de Gagnoa, Cercle du Haut Sassandra, Gagnoa, le Chef de Subdivision Aoust (30 June).

_____. Rapport Politique, 1918.

_____. Rapport d'Ensemble, 1917.

_____. Rapport d'Ensemble: Enseignement, 1916.

_____. Organisation Administrative, 1915, Cercle des Lagunes: Dabou, Alépé, Bingerville, Abidjan.

_____. Rapport Politique du 4e trimestre de l'année 1914, Abidjan (18 January).

_____. Rapport d'Ensemble: Enseignement, 1915.

_____. Situation Politique, 1915.

_____. Rapport Politique, Cercle de Grand Lahou, Colonie de la Côte d'Ivoire, 15, 4e trimestre 1914 (31 December). In Rapports Politiques du Cercle de Lahou, 1913–1915.

_____. Rapport Politique du 3e trimestre 1914 (5 November).

_____. Rapport Politique, 1914, Cercle des Lagunes (October).

_____. Rapport Politique et de Tournées, Colonie de la Côte d'Ivoire, Cercle de Lahou, District de Divo. 1914 (September).

_____. Rapport Politique, L'Administrateur du Cercle de Grand Lahou à Monsieur le Gouverneur de la Côte d'Ivoire, Bingerville. 1914 (31 August).

_____. Rapport Politique, Colonie de la Côte d'Ivoire, Cercle de Lahou, Poste de Lakota. 1914 (August).

_____. Rapport Politique Trimestriel, L'Administrateur du Cercle de Grand Lahou à M. le Gouverneur de la Côte d'Ivoire, Bingerville, M. Rouset. 1914 (11 July).

_____. Rapport d'Ensemble: Enseignement, 1914.

_____. Rapport d'Ensemble: Enseignement, 1913.

_____. Rapport Politique, Cercle des Lagunes, Abidjan. 1913 (4 October).

_____. Rapport Politique, Cercle des Lagunes, Administrateur Bouval, Dabou. 1913 (13 July).

_____. Rapport Politique, Cercle des Lagunes, Abidjan. 1913 (10 June).

_____. Rapport Politique, Bingerville, Situation du Pays Attié, 1913 (26 April).

_____. Rapport Administratif, Grand Lahou, 4e trimestre, 1913.

————. Rapport Politique, Bingerville. 1913 (31 January).

————. Situation Politique en 1911, Gouverneur General de l'A.O.F., Dakar. 1912 (26 June).

Jeffries, Leonard, Jr. 1971. Sub-National Politics in the Ivory Coast Republic. Ph.D. dissertation, Columbia University, New York.

Johnson, Walton. 1977. *Worship and Freedom: A Black American Church in Zambia*. London: International African Institute.

Joseph, Gaston. 1917. *La Côte d'Ivoire: Le Pays—les habitants*. Paris: Emile Larose.

Journal Officiel de la République de la Côte d'Ivoire. 1961, 4 March, p. 328.

Jules-Rosette, Bennetta, ed. 1979. *The New Religions of Africa*. Norwood, N.J.: Ablex Publishing Corp.

————. 1975. *African Apostles: Aspects of Ritual and Conversion in the Church of John Maranke*. Ithaca, N.Y.: Cornell University Press.

Kimambo, Israia, and Omari, C. K. 1972. The Development of Religious Thought and Centres among the Pare. In *The Historical Study of African Religions*, eds. T. O. Ranger and I. Kimambo, pp. 111–21. Berkeley and Los Angeles: University of California Press.

Kobben, A. J. F. 1960. Prophetic Movements as an Expression of Social Protest. *International Archives of Ethnography* 69(1): 117–64.

Koffi, Yao. 1971. Les Disciples de William Harris. *Ivoire Dimanche* (Abidjan, Ivory Coast), 11 July, pp. 4–6.

Kopytoff, Igor. 1964. Classifications of Religious Movements: Analytical and Synthetic. In *Proceedings of the 1964 Annual Spring Meeting of the American Ethnological Society* (Symposium on New Approaches to the Study of Religion). Seattle: University of Washington Press.

LaBarre, Weston. 1971. Materials for a History of Studies of Crisis Cults: A Bibliographic Essay. *Current Anthropology* 12(1): 3–44.

Lanternari, Vittorio. 1963. *The Religions of the Oppressed: A Study of Messianic Cults*. New York: Alfred A. Knopf.

Linton, Ralph. 1943. Nativistic Movements. *American Anthropologist* 45: 230–40.

Livingston, Thomas W. 1975. *Education and Race: A Biography of Edward Wilmot Blyden*. San Francisco: Glendessary Press.

Loi-plan de développement économique, social, et culturel pour les années 1967, 1968, 1969, 1970. Loi no. 67–302, 10 July 1967, Ministère du Plan.

Lynch, Hollis R. 1967. *Edward Wilmot Blyden: Pan-Negro Patriot, 1832–1912*. New York: Oxford University Press.

Marty, Paul. 1922. *Etudes sur l'Islam en Côte d'Ivoire*. Paris: Editions Ernest Leroux.

Mbiti, John S. 1970. *African Religions and Philosophies*. New York: Doubleday and Co.

Mouézy, Henry. 1954. Le Christianisme en Côte d'Ivoire. *Cahiers Charles de Foucauld*, 3e trimestre, 91–102.

Musson, Margaret. 1950. *The Prophet Harris: The Amazing Story of Old Pa Union Jack*. Wallington, Surrey: Religious Education Press.

Neveux, M. 1923. *Religion des noirs: fétiches de la Côte d'Ivoire*. Alençon: Imprimerie Laverdure.

Newsletter: Afro-American Religious History Group of the American Academy of Religion. 1980. 5(1).

Niangoran-Bouah, Georges. 1969. Les Ebriés et leur organisation politique traditionnelle. *Annales de l'Université d'Abidjan*, series F, vol. 1, fascicle 1, pp. 51–89.

————. 1967. Calendriers traditionnels et concept de temps. *Bulletin d'Information et de Liaison des Instituts d'Ethnosociologie et de Géographie Tropicale* (Université d'Abidjan) 1: 9–26.

————. 1964. La Division du temps et le calendrier rituel des peuples lagunaires de Côte d'Ivoire. Ph.D. dissertation, Institut d'Ethnologie, Musée de l'Homme, Paris.

O'Dea, Thomas F. 1966. *The Sociology of Religion*. Englewood Cliffs, N.J.: Prentice-Hall.

Ogot, Bethwell A. 1972. On the Making of a Sanctuary: Being Some Thoughts on the History of Religion in Padola. In *The Historical Study of African Religion*, eds. T. O. Ranger and I. Kimambo, pp. 122–35. Berkeley and Los Angeles: University of California Press.

Parrinder, E. G. 1969. *Religion in Africa*. Middlesex: Penguin Books.

————. 1953. *Religion in an African City*. London: Oxford University Press.

Parsons, Talcott. 1963. Introduction to *The Sociology of Religion*, by Max Weber. Translated by Ephraim Fischoff. Boston: Beacon Press.

Paulme, Denise. 1962. *Une Société de Côte d'Ivoire hier et aujourd'hui—les bété*. The Hague: Mouton and Co.

Paulme-Schaeffner, Denise. 1968. Note sur le group Nzima. *Bulletin d'Information et de Liaison des Instituts d'Ethnosociologie et de Géographie Tropicale*. (Université d'Abidjan) 1: 14–15.

Peel, J. D. Y. 1968. *Aladura: A Religious Movement among the Yoruba*. London: Oxford University Press.

Platt, William J. 1934. *An African Prophet: The Ivory Coast Movement and What Came of It*. London: SCM Press.

Premier livret de l'education religieuse à l'usage des missions Harristes. 1956. Paris: M. Herbercq.

Price-Mars, Jean. 1960. *Silhouettes de nègres et de négrophiles*. Paris: Présence Africaine.

Pritchard, John. 1973. The Prophet Harris and Ivory Coast. *Journal of Religion in Africa* 5(1): 23–32.

Ranger, T. O. 1972*a*. *The African Churches of Tanzania*. Historical Association of Tanzania, No. 5. Nairobi: East African Publishing House.

———. 1972*b*. Missionary Adaptation of African Religious Institutions: The Masai Case. In *The Historical Study of African Religion*, eds. T. O. Ranger and I. Kimambo, pp. 221–51. Berkeley and Los Angeles: University of California Press.

———, and Kimambo, Israia, eds. 1972. *The Historical Study of African Religion*. Berkeley and Los Angeles: University of California Press.

Recensement d'Abidjan, 1955. 1960. Résultats Définitifs, République de la Côte d'Ivoire, Direction de la Statistique et des Etudes Economiques et Démographiques, Ministère des Finances, des Affaires Economiques et du Plan.

Recensement Démographique de Bouaké, Juillet–Août, 1958. 1960. Résultats Définitifs, République de la Côte d'Ivoire, Direction de la Statistique et des Etudes Economiques et Démographiques, Ministère des Finances, des Affaires Economiques et du Plan.

Recensement des Centres Urbains d'Abengourou, Agboville, Dimbokro, et Man, 1956–1957. 1960. Résultats Définitifs, République de la Côte d'Ivoire, Direction de la Statistique et des Etudes Economiques et Démographiques, Ministère des Finances, des Affaires Economiques et du Plan.

Repertoire des Villages de la Côte d'Ivoire. 1966. Territoire de la Côte d'Ivoire, Service de la Statistique Générale et de la Mécanographie. Vol. 1 (31 December).

Republic of Liberia Interior Department. 1957. *Traditional History and Folklore of the Grebo Tribe*. Monrovia: Bureau of Folkways Research Series.

Ringgren, Helmer. 1969. The Problems of Syncretism. In *Syncretism*, ed. Sven S. Hartman, pp. 7–14. Stockholm: Almquist and Wicksell.

Rodney, Walter. 1972. *How Europe Underdeveloped Africa*. London: Bogle-l'Ouverture Publications. Reprint. Washington, D.C.: Howard University Press.

Rouch, Jean. 1963. Introduction à l'étude de la communauté de Bregbo. *Journal de la Société des Africanistes* 33(1): 129–202.

Roux, André. 1971. *L'Evangile dans la forêt*. Paris: Les Editions du Cerf.

———. 1950. Un Prophète: Harris. *Présence Africaine*, special issue (8–9) of *Le Monde Noir*, pp. 133–40.

Schnapper, Bernard. 1961. *La Politique et le commerce français dans le Golfe de Guinée de 1838 à 1871*. The Hague: Mouton and Co.

Schoffeleers, Matthew. 1972. The History and Political Role of the M'Bona Cult among the Mang'anja. In *The Historical Study of African Religion*, eds. T. O. Ranger and I. Kimambo, pp. 73–94. Berkeley and Los Angeles: University of California Press.

Scott, Emmett Jay. 1911/1971. Is Liberia Worth Saving? Reprinted in *Apropos of Africa: Afro-American Leaders and the Romance of Africa*, eds. Adelaide Cromwell Hill and Martin Kilson, pp. 375–82. Garden City, N.Y.: Doubleday and Co.

Shack, William A. 1979. Foreword to *African Christianity and Patterns of Religious Continuity*, eds. George Bond, Walton Johnson, and Sheila Walker, pp. 1–8. New York: Academic Press.

Shepperson, George. 1954. The Politics of African Church Separatist Movements in British Central Africa, 1892–1916. *Africa* 24(3): 233–46.

Shick, Tom W. 1977. *Behold the Promised Land: A History of Afro-American Settler Society in Nineteenth-Century Liberia*. Baltimore and London: Johns Hopkins University Press.

Sinda, Martial. 1972. *Le Messianisme congolais—et ses incidences politiques*. Paris: Payot.

Smyth, John Henry. 1896/1971. The African in Africa and the African in America. Reprinted in *Apropos of Africa: Afro-American Leaders and the Romance of Africa*, eds. Adelaide Cromwell Hill and Martin Kilson, pp. 56–67. Garden City, N.Y.: Doubleday and Co.

—————. 1882/1971. Dispatches from the United States Ministers to Liberia, 1863–1906. Reprinted in *Apropos of Africa: Afro-American Leaders and the Romance of Africa*, eds. Adelaide Cromwell Hill and Martin Kilson, pp. 108–12. Garden City, N.Y.: Doubleday and Co.

Sundkler, Bengt G. M. 1948. *Bantu Prophets in South Africa*. London: Lutterworth Press. Reprint. Oxford University Press, 1961.

Talmon, Yonina. 1969. Pursuit of the Millennium: The Relations between Religious and Social Change. In *Sociology and Religion: A Book of Readings*, eds. Norman Bernbaum and Gertrud Lenger. Englewood Cliffs, N.J.: Prentice-Hall.

Terray, Emmanuel. 1969. L'Organisation sociale des Dida de Côte d'Ivoire. *Annales de l'Université d'Abidjan*, series F, vol. 1, fascicle 2.

Thirty Thousand African Christians without a Pastor. 1924. *Foreign Field*, December, pp. 59–62.

Thompson, E. W. 1928. The Ivory Coast: A Study in Modern Missionary Methods. *International Review of Missions* 17(68): 630–44.

Trichet, Pierre. 1971. Des églises prophétiques en Afrique noire. *Les Peuples du Monde* 39 (March): 23–38.

Turner, Harold W., ed. 1970. Bibliography of Modern African Religious Movements—Supplement 2. *Journal of Religion in Africa* 3(3): 161–208.

———. 1968. Bibliography of Modern African Religious Movements—Supplement 1. *Journal of Religion in Africa* 1(3): 173–210.

———. 1966a. *History of an African Independent Church: The Church of the Lord (Aladura)*. 2 vols. London: Oxford University Press.

———. 1966b. A Methodology for Modern African Religious Movements. *Comparative Studies in Society and History* 8(3): 281–94.

Turner, Henry McNeal. 1893/1971. *African Letters*. Nashville, Tenn.: A.M.E. Sunday School Union. Reprinted in *Apropos of Africa: Afro-American Leaders and the Romance of Africa*, eds. Adelaide Cromwell Hill and Martin Kilson, pp. 266–80. N.Y.: Doubleday and Co.

Urbanisme et modernisation de l'habitat rural en Côte d'Ivoire. 1967. Ministère de l'Information de la République de Côte d'Ivoire, Abidjan.

van Bulck, G. 1961. Le Prophète Harris vu par lui-même. *Devant les Sectes Non-Chrétiennes, Section Missiologique, Museum Lessianum* 41: 120–24.

van Steenkiste, Guy. 1971. Pense ce que tu sens. *Fraternité Matin*. Abidjan, 2 November.

Vidal, Claudine. 1966. Passé et présent des innovations religieuses au Congo Léo. *Le Mois en Afrique*, 5 May, pp. 61–77.

Voget, Fred W. 1956. The American Indian in Transition: Reformation and Accommodation. *American Anthropologist* 58(2): 249–63.

Wach, Joachim. 1944. *Sociology of Religion*. Chicago: University of Chicago Press.

Wade, Abdoulaye. 1968. *La Doctrine économique du mouridisme*. Dakar: L'Interafricaine d'Editions.

Walker, Frank Deauville. 1927a. More about the Prophet Harris. *Foreign Field*, March, pp. 136–41.

———. 1927b. The Prophet Harris, Found at Last. *Foreign Field*, February, pp. 107–12.

———. 1926. *The Story of the Ivory Coast*. London: Cargate Press.

Walker, Sheila S. 1980a. Witchcraft and Healing in an African Christian Church. *Journal of Religion in Africa* 10(2): 127–38.

———. 1980b. Young Men, Old Men, and Devils in Aeroplanes: The Harrist Church, the Witchcraft Complex, and Social Change in Ivory Coast. *Journal of Religion in Africa* 11(2): 106–23.

———. 1979a. The Message as the Medium: The Harrist Churches of the Ivory Coast and Ghana. In *African Christianity: Patterns of Religious*

Continuity, eds. George Bond, Walton Johnson, and Sheila S. Walker, pp. 9–64. New York: Academic Press.

―――. 1979*b*. Women in the Harrist Movement. In *The New Religions of Africa*, ed. Bennetta Jules-Rosette, pp. 87–97. Norwood, N.J.: Ablex Publishing Corp.

―――. 1977. Religion and Modernization in an African Context: The Harrist Church of the Ivory Coast. *Journal of African Studies* 4(1): 77–85.

―――. 1975. Review of *The Prophet Harris* by Gordon Mackay Haliburton. *International Journal of African Historical Studies* 8, supp. A: 73–79.

―――. n.d. African Initiative and Indigenous Christianity in Ivory Coast. Unpublished manuscript.

Wallace, Anthony F. C. 1966. *Religion: An Anthropological View*. New York: Random House.

―――. 1956. Revitalization Movements. *American Anthropologist* 58: 264–81.

Weber, Max. 1963. *The Sociology of Religion*. Boston: Beacon Press.

―――. 1958. *The Protestant Ethic and the Spirit of Capitalism*. New York: Charles Scribner's Sons.

―――. 1947. *The Theory of Social and Economic Organization*. New York: Oxford University Press.

Webster, James Bertin. 1964. *The African Churches among the Yoruba, 1888–1922*. London: Oxford University Press.

Welbourn, F. B. 1961. *East African Rebels: A Study of Some Independent Churches*. London: SCU Press.

―――, and Ogot, B. A. 1966. *A Place to Feel at Home*. London: Oxford University Press.

Wilson, Monica. 1971. *Religion and the Transformation of Society: A Study of Social Change in Africa*. Cambridge: Cambridge University Press.

Worsley, Peter. 1968. *The Trumpet Shall Sound*. New York: Schocken Books.

Yando, Emmanuel. 1970. L'Evolution du Harrisme en Côte d'Ivoire. Bachelor of Theology thesis, Faculté de Théologie Protestante, Paris.

Yegnan, Touré. 1968. Autorité familiale et autorité politique dans un village ebrié (Songon-M'Bratté). *Bulletin d'Information et de Liaison des Instituts d'Ethnosociologie et de Géographie Tropicale* (Université d'Abidjan) 1(2): 13.

Zolberg, Aristide. 1969. *One Party Government in the Ivory Coast*. Princeton, N.J.: Princeton University Press.

Index

78; received Harris's cane-cross, 78; test of faith, 78; assisted by Ebrié men, 81; spectacular conversions, 82; stopped at gunpoint, 82; success of, 82; presiding over Harrist Church, 84; praised for leadership, 84, 86; faith of, 90; special distinction of, 93; as a prophet, 104; continuing the mission, 117; visit to Liberia, 122; as leader of Harrists, 128; development of church structure, 145; Harris's successor, 146

Aladura church, 159

Alcohol, 91, 114; and alcoholism, 110

Alladian, 22, 24, 49, 117

Alland, Alexander, analysis by, 154

All Saints Day, 90, 108, 128, 130

Altars, 26, 41

American Colonization Society, 3

American Protestant Episcopal mission, 14

Amos-Djoro, Ernest, 63, 92, 173 (n. 8)

Ancestors, respect for, 111; disobedience of, 135; powerful and sovereign, 139

Angel Gabriel, 18, 155

Angoulvant, Governor Gabriel, 32, 46

Animists, 126, 127

Annuaire Nationale de la Côte d'Ivoire, 126

Anono: celebration in, 90; village of, 109, 122; religious groups in, 117

Apostles, 45, 86, 91, 94, 121, 149; selection of, 94; council of, 111

Archbishop, 86

Armed force, 164

Armstrong, 172 (n. 4)

Ascension, 108

Assinie, 28, 33, 35, 42

Atcho, Albert, 112, 130, 134; his role in Harrist Church, 173 (n. 7)

Attié, 22, 117

Audoin, 39

Authority, respect for, 107

Avikam, ethnic group, 22, 26

Awaiting the teachers, 74, 136

Axim, 46

Baptism, 92, 158; power of, 39, 40; Harris's commands regarding, 41; meaning of, 41, 161; no pay for, 91; dual function of, 134, 160; as act of initiation, 161

Barclay, President Arthur, 14

Barrett, David, xiv, 169 (n. 3), 170 (n. 4)

Bas-Cavally, 36

Bassam, 35, 42

Bayibo, the village of, 26

Behavioral continuity, 160

Bell ringers, 102

Bells, to summon congregation, 96

Benediction, 103

Benoit, Pierre, 18, 53, 66, 69, 74, 77, 125; his visit, 65; his journal, 65, 67; image of, 75; visit to Liberia, 146, 149; refers to Harris, 153; his report, 171 (n. 10)

Beugré, 26, 154, 158

Bianquis, Jean, 51, 65, 107, 153, 172 (n. 1)

Bible, 15, 39, 57, 62, 67, 73, 78, 99, 101, 107, 109, 114, 126, 130, 170 (n. 4); power of, 158; quoted concerning polygamy, 172 (nn. 5, 6). See also Gospel; Word of God

Biblical understanding, 124

DATE DUE

DEC 1 5 2005			